GODLY
PLAY

Jerome W. Berryman

GODLY PLAY

An Imaginative Approach
to Religious Education

Augsburg
MINNEAPOLIS

Library of Congress Cataloging-in-Publication Data

Berryman, Jerome.
    Godly play : an imaginative approach to religious education / Jerome W. Berryman.
        p.   cm.
    Originally published: San Francisco : HarperSanFrancisco, 1991.
    Includes bibliographical references and index.
    ISBN 0-8066-2785-9
    1. Christian education—Philosophy.   2. Play—Religious aspects—Christianity.   I. Title.
    [BV1464.B47   1995]
    268'.01—dc20   94-38496
                                                                    CIP

Manufactured in the U.S.A.   AF 9-2785
99   98   97   96   95   1   2   3   4   5   6   7   8   9   10

Contents

Acknowledgments

First, I would like to express my gratitude to my teacher Sofia Cavalletti of Rome. She is the leading figure in the third generation of those working in the area of religious education that I call "Godly Play" and she calls "The Catechesis of the Good Shepherd." My own work does not attempt to duplicate her tremendous contributions. Instead, I have tried to experiment with and extend what she has already achieved. This book is an introduction to my fourth generation efforts along this line.

Since this book is an introduction to my life work, it is appropriate that I pay special tribute to those who gave me life. I dedicate this book to Louise Cauthers Berryman and Jerome C. Berryman, my parents. I thank them for their heritage, their lives, and especially for their patience with their first-born.

My sister, Merilyn, and my brother, Tom, and their families have had a hand in this too. It is much more complicated today because of geographical distances, but we still play.

The people of the First Presbyterian Church in Ashland, Kansas, need to be remembered. The stern Presbyterians not only taught me how to work but how to smile. In 1959 they sent me off to seminary at Princeton, an experience and a beginning that I would not trade for anything.

Thea, my truest and most favorite playmate, and I were married in 1961. Being with her turns work into play and her deep knowledge of children and teaching informs the process this book is about at every level. Our girls, Alyda and Coleen, clearly have picked up the seriousness of play as well. Now, even our son-in-law, Michael, and our granddaughter, Alexandra, have made important contributions to its continuing spirit.

Two people had a special professional influence on this book. They are Professor John Dominic Crossan and Professor Werner Kelber. They read my manuscript for a book about children and parables years ago, and took it so seriously that I put it aside to mature. Later, I realized that it was part of a larger idea I had in mind. An introduction to the whole project was needed. This is that introduction.

What would you do if someone sent you a bundle of a book in the mail and asked you to read and comment on it? No one has that much free time; the work is too hard. Those who took up this task with good cheer are: Locke Bowman, Sofia Cavalletti, Jim Fowler, Steve Gutstein, Maria Harris, John Hull, Jim Loder, Berard Marthaler, Clarence Snelling, and John Westerhoff. Our friendships seem to have survived my request, so I thank them not only for their help but especially for the friendship it represents.

The people of Augsburg Books deserve a special note of appreciation. They continued to believe in this book even after its first edition was sold out. Their republishing of it is a powerful statement of their own commitment to making available the best possible resources for those who care about the spiritual development of children and families.

I know, you're thinking, "He's even going to thank the dog!" Yes, there is always a dog nearby, but the dog who helped me the most, an old friend of seventeen years, died before the book was finished. He used to crawl under the desk and sleep on my feet during the late night hours. Thanks, Goat.

Jerome W. Berryman

Preface

This book is about religious growth and how to foster it. If the language of religion can be associated with the creative process, it can help with one's life pilgrimage. If religious language is learned in a way that links it to raw authority, shame, guilt, fear, or some other destructive association it can cripple us and stop religious growth in its tracks.

I remember working with the child of a family that was very religious. Each week the people at the therapeutic nursery school, who asked for the consultation, saw improvement in the child. On Monday, after spending the weekend with his family, the little boy was again withdrawn, hitting other children, and angry.

A visit to the child's church helped explain the rhythm of improvement and relapse. Each Sunday the child got an intense dose of repressive, angry, and shame-producing religious communication that was supported by his parents. This powerful communication went to the core of the child's awareness of himself and the world. It was no wonder that he was so demoralized on Monday mornings.

The little boy's parents did not set out to stunt the religious growth of their child. They were doing what they thought was best and they stuck to it. This was a case of the best intentions gone awry. The way to prevent such unintentional mistakes is not to avoid altogether the issues of religion with children. This teaches by default that you do not value religion. What we need to do is to learn more about what religion is and how to use its special language appropriately.

Religious language does something for us that no other kind of communication can do as well. Like the languages of law, ethics, medicine, and art, it has a special job to do. The task of religious language is to help us take "the big picture" into consideration.

The big picture is framed on one side by the boundary that limits and defines us by death. Another limit that defines us and our view of the world is our need for meaning. A third limit is the threat of freedom. It is a threat because we often don't want to take responsibility for what we can freely choose to do. The big picture is framed on the fourth side by the limit of being alone. We come into life alone and must make our own exit. This is an existential issue and not ordinary loneliness.

Many people think that children do not have an awareness of these existential limits. Often adults prefer to think that children are always happy. It puts much less pressure on us as adults and relieves us of having to face such issues ourselves.

This book proposes that children *do* have an awareness of the existential limits to their being and their knowing and that they are crying out in ways we do not often recognize for the language tools to help them build a life that takes such ultimate concerns into consideration. I say this because when children engage in Godly play they often become deeply happy as if some great need has been satisfied.

Of course, children do not use adult language to speak of their encounters with the existential boundaries to life. They certainly do not divide their ultimate concerns into such neat concepts as I have suggested above. This makes it all the more important for us to notice such issues in the lives of children and to give them religious language to name, value, and express their ultimate concerns so they can cope with them now and prepare for a more healthy and creative life later.

The Christian language system is the one I know best, so my remarks in this book about Godly play are somewhat confined to this tradition. Despite my own limitations, I think much of what is said here can be applied to other religious traditions.

My book proposes to do many things. I want to draw you into Godly play so you can know it from the inside. I also want to describe it from the outside so you can recognize it when you see it practiced by others. I want to talk to teachers of young children and parents as well as to students of theology and their professors.

I think that authors often underestimate what teachers and parents want to know about religious education and overestimate the experience that professors have with children. This book weds the theory of the professors with the experience of the teachers and parents for the benefit of all.

The book begins by talking about the importance and structure of religious communication. Laughter and playfulness combined with an attention to structure are necessary in order for Godly play to work. Laughter, playfulness, and structure are especially important for *teaching* the art of such communication.

The second and third chapters of the book expand on what the experience of Godly play is like. In the second chapter I talk about how it feels to me. In the third chapter I make an estimate of what Godly play is like for children by describing the work of two boys with the parable of the Mustard Seed over twelve weeks.

A good bit of religious education literature is devoted to describing lessons for teachers to use. Chapters four and five are about the spoken and unspoken aspects of the kind of lessons that draw one into Godly play. One needs to make such lessons personal and to use the whole learning environment to support the creative process for such lessons to teach how to use religious language well.

One of the major assumptions of this book is about the importance of the imagination-in-action, the creative process. The sixth chapter is devoted to a description and discussion of the imagination in relation to Godly play.

Godly Play draws to a close by discussing religious language in more detail. Finally, a case is made for the discovery of the Creator in the creative process. This is a very human and natural form for our pilgrimage to take, for, as it says in Genesis, we are made in the Creator's image.

1 Playing and Reality

Godly play has something in common with all play. The pleasure of it comes from the act of playing itself. Play is re-creation. The enormous range and depth of such re-creation, however, is too often overlooked. Many see playing as a superficial or trivial act, but I see it as a life-giving act. It makes us young when we are old and matures us when we are young.

Playing can't be done without a structure. Structure enables people to play together and is needed even for a solo game. Consequently, any discussion of playing needs to include something about games as well as about the nature of play. This is especially important when we are discussing Godly play, because many games begin in a playful way but move by degrees into work and end in self-destruction. Godly play must remain play to be Godly, so let us begin by looking for a game worth playing.

A GAME WORTH PLAYING

Imagine that you and three other people are sitting around a table. I join you and put a carved wooden box down in the middle of the tabletop. I unfasten the elaborate brass latch and slowly open the box. First, I take out a stopwatch and a bell and set them on the table. I wind the stopwatch. It begins to tick. Next, I pass the box around the table and ask each of you to select one of the balls inside. The box is full of balls of all sizes and colors, made of materials ranging from rubber to fragile glass. I also invite you to select seven small wooden figures from those in the box. There are trees, cars, animals, houses, and many other small images of the world's artifacts.

"Let's play a game," I say with a smile. "You are the players. I am the game master, the *magister ludi*. I will start and end the game with the bell. The stopwatch will keep the time. I see you all have your game pieces. Ready now? Begin!"

I ring the bell. The timer is ticking away. You and the other people at the table look at each other. The game has begun, but what are you supposed to do? You bounce your ball in a tentative way, up and down, in front of you. Another person moves her playing pieces around in different designs. A third person puts his ball inside a small, tight circle of playing pieces.

There is an awkward pause. Everyone is uncertain about whether or not to talk. The person across from you bounces his ball your way. You bounce it to another person. She holds it and gives her ball to the person next to her. That person keeps the ball but passes some of his wooden objects to the one who made the first interpersonal "move" of the game. Suddenly, the bell rings.

"The game is over," I say. "How did you like it?"

No one speaks. You feel a mild sense of discomfort. The person across the table fidgets with frustration. Suddenly, a third person shows anger. He feels that he has been taken advantage of and made to appear foolish. He says, a bit too loudly, "What kind of 'game' is this, anyway?"

"Maybe it is not a game," I say softly. "Perhaps something was missing. Let's take an inventory. There were (1) *players* (you and the others sitting at the table); (2) *game pieces,* the objects of value the game is played with (the wooden figures and the balls); (3) *time* for the game (the time kept by the timer and marked by the bell); and (4) *place* (the table). What was missing?"

The main cause of the players' frustration was the lack of a goal for the game. People can't play a game together if they do not share a common goal. The players began to search for a common goal when they intuited the need for it, but they were just beginning to work something out when the "non-game" came to an end. If it had gone on longer, a complete game might have developed.

A second element missing from the incomplete game structure was a set of *rules* to give order to the playing so that a common goal might be reached (once that had been established). Rules organize the play and reduce the random conflict that can develop and distract the players from moving toward the game's goal.

If we understand games as human activities that have the six characteristics just mentioned, then we can see that games are everywhere. Games are sometimes silly and superficial, but they can be very, very serious even to adults. In 1970 Clark C. Abt published a book called *Serious Games*,[1] in which he discussed how games can unite seriousness of thought with important problems. For example, he discussed educational games for math, social studies, and other school subjects; war games and games for occupational choice and training; and games for planning and problem solving in government and industry. Games such as these do more than entertain. This is not to say, however, that games can't be *both* entertaining *and* serious. They can be.

What, then, is a game? Abt wrote: "A game is an *activity* among two or more independent *decision-makers* seeking to achieve their *objectives* in some *limiting context.*"[2] This definition is so broad that it raises another question: What is *not* a game? Noncompetitive processes such as production lines are not games; nor are predetermined procedures.

We can better recognize the activities that deserve to be called games by exploring some common features of games. For example, while all games simulate something from the real world, not all simulations are games. A computer's simulation of traffic flow or chemical reactions is not a game, because the outcomes are predetermined by the computer program. There is no possibility of either winning or losing in the outcome, only a set of results. Games that simulate coordinations of actions in the real world can help train us for the real thing.

Games can also frame our coordinations of actions, much as the stage frames a play, so that we can become involved emotionally to discover more about ourselves and life itself. When an actor on stage points a gun at us, we know it is a play, so we can attend to our feelings. Outside on the street, if someone points a gun at us we'd better duck without musing about it. Similarly, when we engage in therapy, action is suspended by the game structure so self-reflection can take place to inform our action.

Although games involve competition, competition in a game does not have to be between players. A mountain-climbing team can compete together against the difficulty of the rock and weather. People also compete against themselves in games, even games played with others, to achieve their personal best.

Different game goals require different kinds of competition. Among life games, for example, there are games we play for material things, and there are "metagames," which we play for intangibles.[3]

Tangible goals are sought in coordinations of actions such as the Glory Game, the Fame Game, and the Money Game. I don't need to describe such games in detail; we are all familiar with them. They all have a product—a tangible result that can be "won"—but the product does not satisfy the player. The focus is on the quantity of things, not the quality of the experience. As a result, playing these games leads to the need to accumulate more of what the game is played for. Play turns into work and finally into self-destruction.

There are two intermediate kinds of games between the games with tangible goals and those with intangible goals. Some people opt out of all life games and play what might be called the No Aim Game. Its goal is to have no aim in life. The other intermediate game is the Householder Game. Its goal is to raise a family.

Metagames are played for the quality of the experience rather than the quantity of things to be accumulated. One such game is the Art Game, which is played for beauty. A second example is the Science Game, which is played for knowledge. The Religion Game is played in an approved organization, a church, in a formal way for the payoff, "salvation." Among metagames, though, the game most worth playing is played with God. This game is the Godly Game. It is played for its own sake, whether it is played in a church or elsewhere.

The difference between the Religion Game and the Godly Game needs some clarification. They are often confused, because a church organization might be involved in either game. The experience of the German Augustinian monk and later Reformation leader Martin Luther (1483–1546) can help us describe the difference.

Luther was afflicted with what he called *Anfechtung,* a German word so important and so difficult to translate that Roland Bainton expanded on its meaning in this way: "It may be a trial sent by God to test man, or an assault by the Devil to destroy man. It is all the doubt, turmoil, pang, tremor, panic, despair, desolation and desperation which invade the spirit of man."[4] Luther struggled with this overwhelming experience in a religious way according to what the church had at hand as tools for him to use.

First Luther used the approach of self-help. Bainton noted Luther's comment about this: "I was a good monk, and I kept the rule of my order so strictly that I may say that if ever a monk got to heaven by his monkery it was I." The trouble was that despite nearly killing himself with his vigils, prayers, reading, and other work, he had no sense of peace or of a creative relationship with the Creator.

Luther also tried to rely on the merits of the saints. In 1510 he and another brother were sent to Rome to represent the Augustinian order in Erfurt, where he was living as a monk. In Rome there were more possibilities for indulgences than anywhere. For example, more indulgences were given for traveling between the Lateran and St. Peter's in the same city than were awarded for a pilgrimage to the Holy Land. Luther returned from the Eternal City more troubled than when he had left. Bainton tells us that Luther said "he had gone to Rome with onions and had returned with garlic."

He also tried the way of confession. When Luther returned from Rome, he was sent to the Augustinian cloister in Wittenberg, a new university town. It was there that he met the vicar of the order, Johann von Staupitz. No one could have been a better spiritual guide, as we shall see in a moment. Luther would confess for six hours at a time. Finally, the confessor

grew weary and said, "Man, God is not angry with you. You are
angry with God. Don't you know that God commands you to
hope?" Such a command was of little use to Luther, for he was
sure his memory was hiding some sin or else that he did not
even recognize some act as important for confessing. He knew
that for a sin to be forgiven it had to be confessed, but he was
not sure when his list was complete.

Staupitz was a mystic. He had experienced God. His knowledge of God allowed his own restlessness to rest. Luther's experience of God was so conflicted and distorted that he knew
nothing about God but anger or silence. His spiritual life was
dry. The abyss was a place of terror. There was no creative way
for Luther's rebellion to meet the Creator.

Finally, Staupitz informed Brother Martin that he would
study for his doctor's degree and that he would begin preaching and counseling. He would also begin to teach Bible at the
university. Luther stammered that all that work would kill him.
Staupitz did not react. He set Brother Martin to work.

Soon Luther was too busy to practice religion for the
payoff, salvation. He began to enjoy his work, serious though
he was. He struggled to know what the Psalms meant and what
the Gospels were talking about. He improved his Greek and began to be conscious of the many shades of meaning in the
Greek of Paul's letters.

While working on lectures for Paul's letter to the Romans, Luther broke through to an awareness about God that
he could not win by approaching God directly by pathways the
church had found useful for others. Luther had to find his
own way. The word *justice* in Greek had two meanings, he discovered. In English the two meanings would be translated
"justice" and "justification." "Justice" was what Luther had
felt, a sentence pronounced for failure, rendering a punishment. That is what the Latin text had told him was the only
meaning. In contrast, the "justification" also referred to by
the Greek text pointed toward a process. In this sense, justice
is served when a judge suspends a sentence and places the prisoner on parole. Confidence and personal interest are expressed for the prisoner, and there is an expectation that he
or she will become a new person. Through his discovery of

justification, Luther learned that faith is not an achievement, a work product. It is a gift.

Luther came close to God indirectly as he played the game of preparing his lectures, thinking about his students, praying over his preaching, and being involved in pastoral care. Ironically, his personal path toward God became normative for the church he established. What had been a kind of play for him later became a kind of work for others, because it was a required path.

What Luther had found was Godly play. Godly play is the playing of a game that can awaken us to new ways of seeing ourselves as human beings. It is the way to discover our deep identity as Godly creatures, created in the image of God. The possibility of Godly play puts the games played for glory, fame, and wealth, for "no aim," for home and family, for art or science, and even for salvation into a new and astounding frame. This larger frame, staked out at the limits of our being and knowing, reveals how limited the other games are and how they turn play into work so that the player winds down into self-destruction.

How do I know this claim about Godly play is true? How can you test this proposition? The only way to know whether a game exists is to engage in the game. It is a matter of winning and losing. One must actually play the Godly Game to know.

The winning and losing of games is important, because a proper balance is necessary for a game to remain a game even if it has all six of the structural elements mentioned earlier. A game that is too easily won presents no challenge. It does not stimulate one's interest. A game that can never be won overwhelms one's interest. Commitment to a game one always wins destroys the *game*. Commitment to a game one can never win destroys the *player*.

Godly play is a way to know God. The problem is that, paradoxically, if we play at Godly play to know God rather than for its own pleasure, we will not become aware of God as a player. Instead, like Luther, we will see God as an alien and even angry Other. Playing the ultimate game as if it were instrumental to reach some goal other than itself excludes us from the very knowledge we seek. Playing the ultimate game to know God makes the player awkward and judgmental. Playing for the pleasure of playing itself makes the player graceful so that God, the player, other players, and God's earth all can join in the game.

The *goal* of Godly play is to play the ultimate game for itself. The *players* are God, the self, others, and nature. The *place* for play is at the edge of knowing and being. The *time* has a very clear limit. It is our lifetime. The *pieces of value* in the game are the "pieces" of religious language by which we play. The *rules* that shape the play are found in the pattern of the creative process in communication with the Creator.

The example of Martin Luther's journey toward God shows us something else in addition to the distinction between the Religion Game and the Godly Game. It suggests that Staupitz must have smiled in his care for Brother Martin and that Luther's laughter became deeper and more spontaneous as he grew less angry and more given to talking theology around the table. Luther had shifted from a religion of work and anger to a religion of joy and deep play.

But what is this "deep play" that is so joyful? Playing is fundamental to our identity as human beings, so let's take a closer look at what it involves and what this means for Godly play.

PLAYING

Let's begin where we all begin, with mothers and babies. One of the world's greatest observers of mothers and babies was Donald W. Winnicott (1896–1971). Let's make his view of the connection between playing and reality and mothers and babies our starting point.

Winnicott was born in Plymouth, England, and went to Jesus College, Cambridge, in 1914. He read medicine, but his medical studies were interrupted by World War I. In 1917 he was accepted as a surgeon probationer on a destroyer, the only medical officer and one of the youngest men on board. The ship saw combat, and Winnicott was proud that he had contributed.

After the war Winnicott resumed his education and by 1920 was a qualified doctor specializing in what was then called children's medicine. He had always shared with his sisters what was regarded as a family talent for getting along with children, and all through his training the problems of children interested him most. His colleague, the pediatrician Jack Tizard, wrote in his obituary of Winnicott, "To say that he understood children would to me sound false and vaguely patronizing: it was rather that children understood him."[5]

In 1919 Winnicott read Freud's *Interpretation of Dreams.* This prompted him to add a new vocation to medicine, the study of psychoanalysis. He undertook this study, naturally, with reference to children as well as adults.

In 1940 Winnicott was appointed psychiatric consultant to the Government Evacuation Scheme in the County of Oxford. The children of England were being moved out of the cities and away from their families to save them from the bombing raids of World War II. His work during the war years with psychotic adult patients and homeless children focused his attention on issues that became central to his contribution. What is important for Godly play is that he found much in common between the playfulness of what he called "good enough mothering" and the playfulness required for good therapy or growth in adults.

Winnicott's pleasure in his work showed in his writing. He had little patience for the mysterious, arcane language other psychoanalysts used, and developed only a handful of idiosyncratic terms—*holding, using, playing, feeling real, illusion and disillusion, true and false self, transitional phenomena.* Winnicott used them to stay as close as possible to the lived experiences and to be as understandable as possible to the greatest number of people.

Winnicott respected anyone he was involved with, children or adults. He worked to help patients discover early developmental needs that had been unacknowledged. The most important moments occurred when the client was surprised. These were moments, he thought, when the patient was released from compliance to the needs of someone else and discovered his or her own needs. We shall return later in this chapter to the laughter or smile of recognition that goes with such a surprise.

Winnicott published *Playing and Reality*[6] the same year he died, 1971. When he began his work, psychoanalysis was interested in the interpersonal relations between people and the inner reality of each individual. By the time of his death a new interest had developed in an intermediate area of experiencing to which inner reality and external life both contribute. This intermediate area is a kind of "resting place" in the continual struggle to keep inner and outer reality separate but related. As we shall see, it is especially important for Godly play.

The newborn infant is an unconnected set of feeling states and impressions. The mother holds the child in her mind as well as in her arms and gives form to this chaos by bathing, cooing, naming, rocking, feeding, changing, and all the other things that mothers do with babies. The mother, Winnicott suggested, has a special intuition that can anticipate what the baby needs. This phase lasts some weeks or even longer until the mother's own needs begin to take over again. The baby does not need perfection. During this time the baby needs "good enough" mothering.

The newborn senses a need such as the desire to be fed. The child imagines the satisfaction of the hunger and at the same time the mother intuits the child's need and feeds her baby. As a result the child experiences a sense of omnipotence, a magical joining of desire and satisfaction. It is this sense that gives the child a sense of "me," a sense of reality. The illusion begins that there is an external reality that corresponds to the infant's own capacity to create.

When the mother's period of special sensitivity to the child's needs begins to wane, the satisfaction of needs lags. After all, the child has demanded almost all of the mother's life in the service of its development. Frustration begins for the child. A gap opens between desire and satisfaction. Out of this disillusionment a sense of "not me" arises. The child experiences something new: the mother is out there, independent of me. The mother becomes an object. Reality is taking shape in terms of its subjective and objective aspects.

Winnicott noticed that between the subjective and objective experience was a neutral area of experience. Transitional objects are the focus of such experience. My own transitional object was a blanket with a satin edge. I remember hearing that I called it something like my "pink blanket," but I do not actually remember the color or the words. What I do remember, even after over half a century, is the texture and warmth of the wool and the smoothness of the edge as I held it against my face to go to sleep and suck my thumb.

The transitional object is neither subjective nor objective alone, but both. The child chooses it and lets it go when it is time, but the experience of the overlapping area in which children and adults play with such objects widens into artistic creativity, religious feeling, dreaming, and many aspects of shared symbols and culture.

Things can go wrong. If a transitional object is not allowed to be enjoyed and left behind as other equivalent objects occupy this overlapping area of experiencing, then negative developments can dominate the child's and subsequently the adult's life. These negative developments include fetishism, lying, stealing, loss of affectionate feeling, drug addiction, and obsessional rituals.

Sometimes a mother cannot put herself at the disposal of her child's development, because her own needs are too great. For example, suppose that mother is depressed. The child will then adjust to the mother's needs rather than to his or her own. When the mother can't respond to the child during the initial period of illusion and omnipotence, the child does not feel real and begins to develop a false self that attends to the needs of the mother and later to the needs of others. The child and then the adult can lose touch with inner needs and with the creative or real self.

The link between playing and reality is of fundamental importance to Winnicott and to what this book has to say about Godly play. Playing takes place in the intermediate and overlapping area of experience between the "me" and the "not me." This area is a place of spontaneity. It is where one does not need to be compliant or acquiescent. We must not organize experience for children down to the last bit of learning, or we extinguish such experiencing. The significant moment in such experiencing is when the child or adult at play surprises himself or herself with a glimpse of the true self.

Godly play is growth-enhancing, because it is a place where one can be not only with the true self but also with the true self of others. Moreover, it is a place that also includes being with the earth and with the Creator God. Godly play, then, is not just for children. It gives us at any age room to make discoveries about a whole web of relationships—with self, others, nature, and God—to nourish us all our life. The quest for this larger reality continues all life long, but the answer does not come to us as a *product* of this creativity. It comes to us as the *process* of the creating itself. The play is the constant and not some formula that reduces this experience to a single part of its process.

This book is more interested in playing itself than in turning play into a teaching device. To make play instrumental is to turn play into work, to demand a product from the activity. The product might be learning this or that lesson the teacher has in mind. This book is about the action in space and time we call playing and struggles against turning playing into a stale, inanimate thing pointed to by the noun "play." It is about teaching the art of playing so one can come close to the Creator who comes close to us and even joins us when we are playing at any age.

In the Christian tradition the central liturgical event, Holy Communion, invites us into the overlapping space to play. Many versions of this liturgy include the phrase that God is in us and that we are in God as we share the bread and wine. We cannot force the experience of God in the intermediate, overlapping area Winnicott located as the place of transitional phenomena. We can only enter the game and play to discover such a presence. This is the kind of play I call Godly play. Teaching the art of such play with religious language is what this book is about.

All of this is well and good, but what about the everyday world? We get involved with all kinds of people who care nothing for us and have no desire to play. All some people can do is take. They are sponges absorbing anything they can from us emotionally, physically, or financially. In the larger world beyond good-enough mothering there are those who interpret an invitation to play only as an imperative to take advantage of those playing as a way of life.

The risk involved in playfulness is why our discussion of games and the search for a game worth playing is so important.

We need to be careful who we play with as well as how we play. The risk of playfulness is also why we need a way to tell when playfulness is present in others and in the structure of a game to see if it is worth playing. One of the ways to tell is to look for deep laughter.

LAUGHING AND PLAYING

There is always a connection between pleasure and true play. Catherine Garvey's book *Play*[7] begins with "the natural history of the smile." Her examination of play in childhood identifies smiling and laughter as important to a playful orientation. The pleasure comes from the sense of mastery and growth we experience in games. The deep pleasure of Godly play comes from the mastery and growth that take place within our human limits by means of our relationship with God, the Creator. This relationship helps us discover our deep identity as creatures who create. This discovery in turn enables us to cope by creating with and transcending the existential limits that both confine and help define us.

Through the centuries, the Christian church has had trouble with laughter. Devout thinkers have debated questions like the following: Did Christ laugh? Is laughter proper to human nature? Can holiness and laughter mix? In general, large organizations, including the church, do not tolerate laughter very well, but in the church laughter has always remained alive somewhere. Where there is laughter there is also play, and where there is play there is the possibility of the Godly Game.

In the late 1940s Hugo Rahner worked on the theological meaning of play. This distinguished Jesuit scholar, the brother of Karl Rahner, published his book *Man at Play*[8] in English in 1965. In it, he reviewed the writings of classical philosophers and theologians up to the synthesis of St. Thomas in the thirteenth century. He argued that this point of view can still inform "the Christian art of life" as we live it today.

St. Thomas rediscovered Aristotle's golden mean applied to playing. Aristotle called people who lived with such balance the *eutrapeloi*, the "well-turning" ones. They are able to turn aptly to laughter, whatever happens to them, without being reduced to flippancy or sarcasm. Thomas counseled that Christians *need* to play and that smiling and laughing are important. He prepared the way for the medieval theology of the merry Christian who sees the limits and inadequacy of all created things and for that very reason can move through life with a theological smile.

The Christians resolved the Greek opposition of comedy versus tragedy into a synthesis of "grave mirth." Various writers before and after St. Thomas have called for this smiling wholeness that integrated the Greek binary view. It was this, Rahner said, that led Clement of Alexandria, the leader of the Alexandrian catechetical school and teacher of Origen in the third century after Christ, to speak of life as a "divine children's game."

The serious and the comic, however, have remained an unstable mixture in the church through the ages. In the culture of the Middle Ages, great forces struggled for balance: high and low station in society, spirit and flesh in personal lives, official and unofficial writings and knowledge, closed and open interpretations of texts, the wise and the foolish. Order and chaos seemed to hang on this balance. Laughter seemed to be the key to order and disorder. If laughter were permitted, then the whole delicate binary structure might fall. It was serious, not comic, to contemplate such a fall . . . at least to some.

Umberto Eco's book *The Name of the Rose*[9] expresses faithfully this medieval conversation and at the same time reflects on the modern conversation about culture and the interpretation of texts. The book's pages abound with many mysteries. There are murders in the Abbey as well as other puzzles for detectives of all kinds to work on. Our concern here is with the disputations between the British Franciscan friar, William of Baskerville, and the Spanish Benedictine, Jorge of Burgos, about laughter.

The Benedictine Rule, which is read at mealtime and studied by novices and monks, is extremely cautious about laughter. Jorge argued that one should say only yes or no, as our Lord commanded. He also said that a word should be used so that it means only one thing. To make pictures and texts that turn things upside down and play with what God has given to us is to lie about creation. Books should be conserved and copied, but all the knowledge that we need has already been given to us by Christ and the Church. Jorge and those like him were convinced that if one is confused an appropriate authority should be found to put the mind at rest.

Franciscans inhabited a very different world. They were not monks in an abbey. They traveled about, and their scholars lived in cities such as Oxford and Paris. The Franciscan friars celebrated a kind of exemplarism. They celebrated the corporeal world as the reflection and expression of the Divine Being. Reality was accessible to them through the senses. The use of playful fiction and images was sanctioned for their spiritual mission.

In the abbey there was a book that Jorge kept hidden: the Second Book of Aristotle's *Poetics*, the book on comedy. The forbidden book was a matter of life and death to Jorge, for if it were discovered, then the tremendous respect for Aristotle as an authority might give comedy and laughter the respect that the Spanish monk feared.

Jorge feared laughter because it foments doubt. Doubt must be resolved by an authority and not by looking at things in a new way. Furthermore, one who is laughing does not believe what is laughed at, but neither does he or she hate it. Jorge had a passion for the truth in all-or-nothing terms. Laughter was of the Devil, who leads us away from truth.

William also had a passion for truth, but his passion had room for laughter. The metaphors, puns, and riddles in literature could be enjoyed for sheer pleasure. They led to speculation about new things and new ways of looking at things. He enjoyed language's many meanings and laughed at his discovery of the answer to the murders in the abbey by the wrong means.

William's laughter was exactly what Jorge feared, for he feared the end of fear. It was fear that kept the whole structure of the passing age in place. Jorge's laughter cracks at the end of the story: "He laughed, he Jorge. For the first time I heard him laugh. . . . He laughed with his throat, though his lips did not assume the shape of gaiety, and he seemed almost to be weeping.''[10] This is the laughter of destruction—of self-destruction—and not the laughter of creation and play.

There is another kind of laughter that is almost as destructive as Jorge's. It is the laughter of the medieval carnival, a carnival that is alive in any age. This is a mocking, deriding laughter that is against all that is high, abstract, spiritual, and holy. This is laughter that is expressed in the spectacle; in parody and abusive language. It is present in the grotesque, the scatological, and the sexual. It is embodied in the false triumph or the reversal of roles in a culture. It pretends to lead us beyond our limits.

Medieval carnival elevated the low and brought the marginal into the center, but only for the time of carnival. Carnival, then, really keeps individuals in their place and only allows them to release some steam at approved times rather than risk imagining a new way to live. When the culture is threatened by chaos, carnival comes to be seen as revolutionary or heretical and is stamped out.

We must learn to distinguish between what is destructively comic and the humor appropriate to the deep laughter that signals Godly play. True humor does not laugh at limits. It understands them. It does not fish for the impossible but knows and accepts the possible. It warns us and reminds us of our cultural limits, but it also smiles about the ultimate limits of humankind and how they can be a gate as well as a grave.

When adults and children encounter the limits to life, there are three kinds of responses: magic, denial, and play. Magic is the attempt to control what is beyond our control and manipulate life's limits by will and belief. Without Godly play, religion can easily be turned into magic. This is the mistake of carnival.

The second kind of response to the limits of human life is denial. We try to control our limits by reason, as if our minds were in complete control of life and death. We pile up layer upon layer of language to give an impression of control. Without Godly play, religion can become a defensive language game of unrelenting seriousness. This was Jorge's mistake.

It is more realistic to approach our limits as William did, except, perhaps, for his intellectual pride. Both directly and indirectly, Jesus pointed to such a response.

Become like a child, he said, if you want to mature as an adult. To play the ultimate game, don't rely on will, belief, denial, or reason alone. Play. Play in a Godly way. Play with the Creator. Enter the existential game with imagination, wonder, and laughter if you want to become new without end.

One of the places the existential game is most explicitly played is in church. There the game is called "worship." In the next section I describe a place for children to learn the art of such play.

WORSHIP AND WORSHIP EDUCATION

Søren Kierkegaard (1813–1855) lived his whole life in Copenhagen. He loved to play along the horizon of his existence and to try to draw that experience into language. Near the end of his life he wrote in his *Journal*, "Thus I sometimes could sit for hours, in love with the sound of speech—when it resounds, that is, with the pregnancy of thought—thus I could sit for whole hours, ah! like a flute-player entertaining himself with his flute."[11]

Kierkegaard loved the theater and suggested that most people think of communication with God in worship as a stage play.[12] In their view, the audience is the congregation. The prompter is God, and the players are the religious leaders—the priests, ministers, rabbis. Kierkegaard proposed that such people had it all wrong. The audience is God. The prompter is the religious leader. The players are the congregation. He was pressing the point that many people do not communicate with God in church but only watch others play at such a game.

Kierkegaard does not go far enough with his image. We are all players—God, congregation, religious leaders, and the building itself—in the language game that takes place in worship. The leader, however, has an added responsibility. He or she performs, to shift the metaphor to the athletic playing field, like an experienced player-coach.

The leader or the member of the congregation might at any time opt out of the game and become a member of the audience. Consciousness easily shifts from being in worship to thinking about what is going on or to merely watching. The

player-coach learns how to do this, going back and forth with
flexibility, as a leader, so others can give themselves completely
to the liturgy and not have to worry about its constructive
benefit, safety, or structure.

We are very careful about the way that we furnish and ar-
range the space in our churches. Time is likewise well considered. Deep feelings are involved in these investments. They
become most evident when changes are proposed for the way
the time or space for worship is arranged.

We will talk much more about religious language and the
ultimate game as this book progresses. What is important to say
now is that the approach to religious education presented here
invites children (and adults) to enter sacred story, parable, and
liturgical action in a seriously playful way, and so to learn the
art of its appropriate use. Immediately the question arises of
where such a game should be played. Is the church the place? Is
a classroom? The answer is that the place needs to be a combination of both.

The place for teaching the art of Godly play is like the
church, but it is not the church. The difference between the
church and the church school, however, is *not* one of tone, feeling, respect, or language. The difference is that the language is
more clearly laid out and materialized in the educational setting. In the educational setting children are not held at a distance. As we shall see, they can grasp the language with their
hands, so they can more deeply grasp it with their lives. When
religious education is conceived of as Godly play and children
are given appropriate means to make meaning and find direction in life and death, then religious education enhances worship and worship enhances religious education.

If play is at the edge of knowing and being, where mystery
begins and limit can end, how can it be brought into a church-
school classroom? Does such talk fail to show proper respect for
religion? How can you make a game of learning to know God?

Such questions are not really new, for others have attempted to fashion images to promote Godly play. Nicholas of Cusa
(Cusanus) was one of these.

Cusanus (1401–1464) was a German cardinal, scholar,
mystic, philosopher, theologian, and reformer who was born at

Cues (Cusa) on the Moselle River. He anticipated the Renaissance in his attitudes toward life and learning. In modern times he influenced Paul Tillich through his early studies for his doctoral thesis. He was rediscovered for our time primarily by Ernst Cassirer.

Cusanus finished the two volumes of *De Ludo Globi* (*The Ball Game*) in 1463. His image of a bowling game in this book and his image of a top spinning in *De Possest* (*On Actualized Possibility*), finished in 1460, are illustrations of his playful intuitions. Cusanus expected the reader to be able to distinguish between the contexts in which serious arguments were made and those where intuition and images prevailed.

Karl Jaspers attempted to describe the ball game of Cusanus in his book *The Great Philosophers:*

> It is played with a wooden ball with a spherical
> hollow off center. When the ball is bowled, it does
> not, since one side is heavier than the other, roll in a
> straight line, but takes a spiral path. The players toss
> the ball over a surface divided into ten concentric
> circles. At the center is the king—Christ. The
> winner is the player whose ball has touched the
> greatest number of circles and comes closest to the
> center.[13]

To construct a place for Godly play in one's imagination or in reality requires the reader to be aware of the limitations of such an enterprise. With a smile, let us proceed. The place we will construct will not be a two-dimensional playing surface like that of Cusanus. Let us imagine together a three-dimensional space, so the game can be "entered" in fact as well as in metaphor.

Let us say that the children will enter a room to learn the art of Godly play. The elements of religious language—sacred story, parable, and liturgical action—are arranged on shelves around the walls. When the room (and communication domain) is entered, the first thing one sees, directly opposite the doorway, is the color of the liturgical season—green, purple, blue, red, white—folded over the center of the focal shelf unit. Resting on this field of color is the Holy Family, made of small wooden figures. Mary, Joseph, a cow, the donkey, the shepherds, sheep, and the Magi all gather around the Christ Child in the manager.

Behind the cluster of figures is a small, upright circle in which the risen Christ holds out his arms. When the Holy Family is presented to the children, we hold up the figure of the Christ Child and say, "Here is the little baby holding out his arms to give you a hug. The baby grew up to become a man. He died, but somehow he is still with us." The baby is then superimposed on the risen Christ. "Now he can give the whole world a hug." The relationship between the Holy Family and the circle of the risen Christ evokes transformation-in-Christ as the core of meaning in the Christian tradition.

To the right of the Holy Family is the Good Shepherd, standing in the gate of a sheepfold full of sheep. These wooden figures rest on a large green circle. On the shelf below the Good Shepherd there is another green circle. On it rests a wooden table. When these two circles are put together on the floor, the figures can be moved from one to the other. This lesson about Holy Communion, created by Sofia Cavalletti,[14] uses one profound symbol of religious language to deepen the liturgical image and vice versa.

To the left of the Holy Family on the top shelf is a white circle upon which rests a substantial white Christ Candle. On the shelf below it is a tray with a basin, a pitcher, a cloth, a prayer book, and a baby doll to baptize. On the third shelf below are candles and other things to celebrate the liturgy of the light, in remembrance of the day the children first received the light of their baptism.

The first set of shelves seen by the entering child not only identifies, names, and values the primary images of Christian identity and transformation but also provides materials that explore the deep identity of Christ at the center of that tradition. "The Good Shepherd" and "The Light" are responses Christ himself made to queries about his own true nature.

In our experimental classroom there are shelf units on either side of the shelf that is the focal point in the room. To the left are materials that invite the child to explore the mystery of Christmas and to the right are materials about the mystery of

Easter. Our research classroom also has a small altar and sacristy area to help children identify, name, and value the objects that help us enter Holy Communion.

When you move toward the liturgical shelves these things become clearer, but let's stop in the middle of the room and turn to our right. A new set of shelves comes into view. The shelf unit along the wall to our right has six guiding parables in golden boxes set out along its top shelf. There is also a box that has "all" (about fifty) of the parables of Jesus typed onto gold cards.

The shelf just below the top shelf with its six gold boxes holds other kinds of parabolic materials. They are not gold, since they are not parables Christ told. The lower shelves of this unit have such things as "parables about parables" and materials about the Beatitudes and the sayings of Jesus. There are also games that can be played to explore individual parables and to see patterns and themes in the whole parable collection.

If we keep turning to our right our gaze next falls on the art shelves, which are on the wall by the door we came in. Here are the paints, paper, clay, markers, watercolors, pencils, wood scraps, wire, and other things children can use to make an art response to the lesson of the day or other lessons they choose to work with. (We say "work" to mean "serious and deep play.") This word also assigns deep play the value that the culture gives to work. Furthermore, any growth-producing activity *is* the child's work.)

If we keep turning to the right our view passes the door again. To its right are some shelves for books. Let's keep right on turning, though, because in this classroom books are of secondary importance, except, perhaps, for children in late childhood. One of the objectives of this approach is to break the trance of the printed page by telling and showing the sacred stories, parables, and liturgical action rather than having children read about them. Sometimes, we are aware, books are used as a defense against becoming involved with the power of religious language.

We come now to the final wall. Here are shelves that hold models of many of the primary sacred stories from Genesis through the New Testament. They materialize Noah and the Flood, Abraham and Sarah, Exodus, and many other sacred stories.

In general this curriculum of materials and presentations is a spiral one. The primary images are on the top shelves. They expand into the extensions and additional lessons nested carefully below. The lower shelves have on them such things as maps, models, time lines, and other supplementary items.

About the center of the sacred story wall is a different kind of shelf. It stands between the Old Testament and the New Testament shelf units. Greek and Hebrew alphabets and lessons are placed there. Even the shapes of the letters in these alphabets tell much about their way of communicating.

This special shelf unit also holds what we call "the desert box." The desert box is a transparent plastic box with a lid, filled with sand. "So many important things happened in the desert," we say, "so, of course, we need a piece of the desert in our classroom." Many of the lessons use this desert box as the focal point for their presentation.

If we turn once more to the right we have turned all the way around and have arrived again at the focal shelf we saw first when we came in the room. We have also turned all the way around within the system of Christian communication and value.

Working within such a place allows children to make sensorial links among all of these images and means of Christian communication. Children at the preoperational and concrete-operational stages of cognitive development, as described by Piaget, can "think" theologically in such a place because the tools are at hand in a sensorimotor way. The careful arrangement and concrete embodiment of the communication system of the Christian tradition makes this kind of thinking possible.

A place like the one we have imagined does exist. It is essentially a description of a model classroom, called The Children's Center. It exists in many other forms in churches of various sizes, amid the push and pull of parish needs and limitations. It is a place in which I have seriously played, wondered, and developed resources and strategies for and with children and the Creator since the early 1970s. It is a place for Godly play.

What is it like to enter such a place? What is the experience of Godly play like? The next two chapters will attempt to answer these questions. In chapter 2 we will enter the environment as an adult through my own experience. We will then attempt to reconstruct what it is like for children to enter such a place in chapter 3.

2 An Adult at Play

When I first began to work on this chapter, I thought it would be the easiest to write. It has been the hardest. I tried all kinds of ways to describe what I thought adults felt and thought while they were involved in Godly play. Concepts, analysis, composite narratives all failed.

The approach you will find here is autobiographical, but that proved to be even harder to write. In general, people can attend to about seven plus or minus two items in their consciousness at once.[1] The intuition's tracking is much broader, so a great deal that informs my teaching I am not, or perhaps am no longer, conscious of. The same is true for any experienced teacher in any method and with any subject matter. This is part of what makes writing about my experience so hard. The other part is that there is too much to write. Both you and I must be satisfied with something much less than a stream-of-consciousness portrayal of what goes on in the classroom.

The first time I taught in a church school was about 1954. It was in the First Presbyterian Church of Ashland, Kansas. My high school teacher, Mrs. Humphreys, insisted that I take over a junior high school class that was mostly boys. I talked mainly about football, basketball, and track, depending on the liturgical season of sport, but I was puzzled and intrigued by the experience. I had something important to say about God and my life, but I did not yet have a deeply satisfying way to say it.

When I went to Princeton Seminary for my theological training, I was invited *not* to take the Christian education class. Apparently, the first few weeks I had been amazingly disrup-

24

tive. Instead, Professor D. Campbell Wyckoff assigned me to a tutorial with him and required me to write a long paper about my own theory of Christian education, which we worked over together. At the time I was mostly unaware of what was going on, but in later years I discovered others, such as Jim Loder, who had developed a love and interest for religious education through one of Cam Wyckoff's skillful interventions.[2]

Thea Schoonyoung, a music student at Westminister Choir College, and I were married in 1961 and lived our first year together in Princeton. In 1962 I graduated, and we drove to Kansas, where I was assistant and then interim minister of the First Presbyterian Church in Hutchinson. Our daughter Alyda was born there, and I included in my expanding duties the teaching of the high school class on Sunday mornings between worship services and working with the youth group on Sunday evenings.

After a brief interlude for graduate school classes in philosophy and literature, we moved to Indiana, where I was a chaplain, teacher, and coach at Culver (1965–1968), a boarding school that in those days had about nine hundred boys. This gave me a real chance to work with high school people, which I loved. Still, I kept wondering what it would be like to begin even earlier with religious education. I had no idea how to do that. Children were so different from adults and adolescents.

Our second daughter, Coleen, was born while we were at Culver. That event added to my awareness of the complexity and critical importance of childhood. Coleen is a spina bifida girl. She was born with an open spine and the resulting paralysis from about the chest down. Today she walks with crutches and braces, gets around Houston on the bus, skis in the winter, rides horses in the summer, and paints all the time.

After another interlude in school, the Tulsa University School of Law (J.D., 1969), I became involved in a business project in Little Rock, Arkansas, where our daughters were enrolled in a fine Montessori School. Thea and I had been "talking kids" since we were married, so we enjoyed going to the school to sit in the observation rooms and watch the teachers and children at their playful work. Perhaps this was the way to do religious education with young children, I thought.

The children were discovering how language and the world fit together. The teacher was a guide. This approach would allow room for what St. Augustine called the "Inner Teacher" to work.

Our family packed up and moved to Bergamo, Italy, where I studied at the Center for Advanced Montessori Studies. Each day I climbed to the Upper City and walked through the gates in the fourteenth-century walls and across the old piazza to the citadel where the course was held. In the morning I practiced working with the educational materials. In the afternoon and evening there were lectures and demonstrations. In between I worked on my notebooks. We lived there during 1971 and 1972.

This was a family affair. Thea and I continued discussing children and education, but she also was getting acquainted with the city and its people. Alyda took ballet and was on the swim team. Coleen became a kind of celebrity, since she was getting about in style with crutches and braces despite her disability.

That winter in Bergamo I met Sofia Cavalletti. I discovered that my dream of shaping a kind of religious education with the Montessori method had already begun to be realized by Maria Montessori (1870–1952) herself. Cavalletti, with her enormous talent and skill as a teacher of children and as a Hebrew scholar had extended this work for the present generation. Years before, Mrs. Humphreys had planted the seeds of a question that Cam Wyckoff raised firmly and formally; now Cavalletti gave me the tools to begin to fashion an answer. It was an answer that would work for me and for the children who taught me how to teach.

We returned to the United States a year later, coming home through Rome and enjoying another visit with Dr. Cavalletti. Our visits and correspondence continue to this day. As might be expected, our styles have developed in somewhat different ways. I was surprised the other day to look around my own research center and discover that there were two materials there that Maria Montessori had originated and two that Cavalletti had originated. The rest had come from my own response to scripture, children, and the presence of God. It was a strange discovery, because I had assumed that all our materials had come from Montessori and Cavalletti. In a way they had, and yet my task has become to probe, explore, and study what they have done more than to reproduce it. There are others who are quite competent to show what Cavalletti and Montessori have done. My task is not at odds with that, only different.

The story is almost finished now. We moved to Cleveland, where I was headmaster of a Montessori school. I built a Montessori middle school and set up a class for children with learning difficulties. It was then that we discovered Coleen had developed additional major health problems, so we searched the country for the best answer. We found it in Houston and moved.

In Houston Thea and I continued to work with children. Coleen found the help she needed at the Texas Medical Center. Alyda flourished as a dancer. I set up a class for nine-through twelve-year-olds in a Montessori school and taught in various other kinds of schools, including a therapeutic nursery school. I served several churches as director of Christian education and continued to experiment with the method I was developing. At the same time I became a resident and then a fellow in a clinical program for medical ethics at the Institute of Religion.

The experience base expanded. Working with the children in several of the Medical Center's hospitals, I developed an approach to pediatric pastoral care. My consulting work included pediatric psychiatry at Texas Children's Hospital and the Crisis Team at Houston Child Guidance. Baylor College of Medicine appointed me an adjunct assistant professor of pediatric pastoral care, and I became assistant professor of theology and ministry at the Institute of Religion. Each year I continued to work in churches and schools. The idea of working full-time in Christian education was still there, but how that would work out remained a puzzle.

In 1984 I began a consultation at Christ Church Cathedral in the area of Christian education, and in January of 1985 I came on the staff full-time. This move solved two puzzles. Some time later I was ordained an Episcopal priest after twenty-four wonderful and deeply meaningful years as a Presbyterian minister. The awareness of this theological and liturgical change in myself had been growing for nearly a decade, but I now realize that the seeds of the change had been planted many decades before.

My continuing research of religious education moved with me when I came to the cathedral. Thea and I continued to see research children from outside the cathedral family on Saturdays. The two- through seven-year-olds come in the mornings for two hours, and the seven- through twelve-year-olds come for two hours in the afternoon during the twelve weeks before Christmas and the twelve weeks before Easter. We also taught fourth- and fifth-graders on Sunday mornings in a typical forty-five minute education hour. That teaching kept me in touch with the realities of the Sunday morning situation in addition to our longer (two-hour) research classes. Our whole church school used this method for children from two years of age through the fifth grade.

Although I left the Cathedral in 1994 it is this classroom that I have in mind as I tried to put into words what I experienced on Sunday mornings. Thea was there too, which made things look easier than they are. She, too, is a master teacher. Her field is music. She continues to develop a curriculum in her field, as I have in mine. We still love to "talk kids," as we have from the beginning.

◇

My situation is a little different from yours, perhaps, because on Sunday mornings I have already been involved in the eight o'clock and the nine o'clock liturgy. I also tell a story to the children at the chancel steps following the nine o'clock liturgy. My preference is to be already sitting in the circle the class will form as the first children are coming into the room, but I usually don't get there in time.

The story is a composite event that simplifies years of experience. Picture twelve six-year-olds forming the circle that is taking shape in our room in the church school. The story will continue through the feast and the good-byes at the end. I don't always get to take as much time with the good-byes as I would like to, since I need to be back in the cathedral for the eleven o'clock liturgy. Here is the story.

GATHERING AND PREPARATION

I come in quietly, slowing down as I go through the door. Over the years, entering the room has become a signal to me to slow down and to quiet down in voice and spirit. It is almost automatic now. Blending in with the children has also become second nature. I get down in the circle so I am at their eye level as soon as possible. An "over-adulted" room takes away from the community of children and their sense that the journey is their own.

I wave at Thea as I go by and smile. She has been guiding the children into the circle as they have come in. As I move to the main set of shelves and sit down in front of them, Thea moves calmly outside the room to help some parents separate from their children.

"Good morning, Nancy. Hi, Will. Come make a circle. Billy, sit here." I put my hand down beside me to my right to show him where. "Sit by me." My voice is a bit firmer this time. "Let's all get ready for the lesson while the other children are coming in.

"Nancy, why don't you sit right across from me? It will help show the other children where the circle is when they come in. Besides, it's fun to see you. How are you this morning?"

Great, wouldn't you know it: here's Robbie already. "Hi, Robbie. Come over here and sit by me. No. Sit on this side. That's the way. Thank you." I like difficult children. They remind me of myself.

Billy and Robbie are such a team. They always seem to come together. They are as ready to teach chaos as I am to teach the lesson. They are born leaders and so bright. The question is, What will they lead people toward with their gifts?

"Where is Mrs. Berryman?" Robbie asks.

Here comes the first game. Robbie loves to split the teachers. He's lost without Thea here to get the game going. It's a good thing we know all about that. We have devoted whole teachers' meetings to such things when we meet each month.

"She'll be here in a minute, Robbie. We are just fine. Let's visit. You need to get ready first, before we can begin the lesson. We all need to be ready. That's the way."

Thea comes in and sits down by the door in a little chair. After a few minutes she gets up quietly and lines up the parable boxes. Another child comes running up with his father. Thea gently but firmly stops him at the door and visits quietly with him until he decompresses. She speaks to the father and tells him good-bye, firmly implying that he need not come into the classroom, as he seemed about to do. The community of children, and the place itself as the children's room, need to be protected.

Thea quietly closes the door. We want everyone to know that church school starts on time. The parents and children will come when they can, but we want them to trust us about the time-keeping. If they can trust us about that, they can trust us about more important things.

"I'm glad to see you this morning. Let's all get ready for the lesson. You have been very patient waiting for everyone to get here. You are good children. It makes me happy to see you." The children mostly sit cross-legged with their hands in their laps. They are settled. They are ready.

THE LESSON

"This morning I would like to show you a parable. Watch carefully where I go, so you will always know where to find this parable when you want to make it your work."

I really love this parable. I get up and move toward the parable shelves. I don't have to pretend. Slow down. Pick it up carefully. Point to the yellow circle on the box. Good. I start back toward the circle.

"Remember to carry the parable box with two hands," I say to the children.

I like this part. I sit down smoothly and put the gold parable box in the middle of the circle. It's theirs as well as mine. We all come equally to the parable to discover what it means for our lives. That's really all I have to teach.

I lean back and sit there for a moment, reflecting but not about anything in particular. Maybe I'm doing what people talk about when they say they are "centering," I muse as I come out of the reflective state.

I lean forward toward the parable box. "Look, it's the color gold! Gold is very valuable." My fingers move along the edges of the box. "Parables are very valuable. Maybe there is a parable inside."

I pick up the gold box and look at it with wonder and amazement. "It looks like a present. You know, parables are like presents. They are presents you already have. You have them even if you don't know you do. They are yours, so you don't have to buy them. You don't have to borrow them or take them from anyone."

I put the box down again and then push it back into the center of the circle. "You don't even have to go anywhere to find them. They are always with you.

"Look, there's a lid on it." I lean back and point to the box in the center of the circle. "Parables have lids on them, too. Sometimes it's very hard to take the lid off a parable so you can know what's inside. Parables are hard to go into. Sometimes you have to take them out and spread them out so you can go into them.

"I know what we'll do! Let's take the lid off and see what's inside the parable box." I pull the box toward me. I lift the lid a little, seeming to struggle a bit to do so, and pull out the yellow felt underlay. The lid still covers most of the box to suggeso the mystery inside and to help the children avoid being distracted by what is still inside.

"Look." I hold up the yellow cloth. It makes a crumpled and strange shape in the air. I put it down on the floor and begin to spread it out. I want to touch every part of the underlay as I smooth it out. It's my way of beginning to enter the parable and to show how much I love it.

"I wonder what this could be? I mean, I wonder what it could really be."

"It could be the sun," Bobby says.

"It looks like a lemon to me," Billy says.

"I like all the yellow," Susie whispers.

"It's hard to know what it is. We need some help. I wonder if there is anything else in the box to help us." I look inside. "Oh, look, here's something. It's a person!"

I put down the cardboard figure at the side of the underlay farthest from me, turned so that it is right-side-up to most of the children. I can turn the figure around in my mind and see it right-side-up, but the little ones can't do that yet.

I go on with the lesson. "There was once someone who did such amazing things and said such wonderful things that people followed him. As they followed him, they heard him talking about a kingdom, but it wasn't like the kingdom they lived in. It wasn't like any kingdom they had ever visited. It wasn't even like any place they had ever heard of. So, they couldn't help it. They just had to ask him, 'What is this kingdom of heaven like?' "

While everyone is looking at the parable, I hide a rolled-up green tree made of felt inside my hand. This is the same hand I will use in a minute to show the children the tiny mustard seed on my extended first finger.

"One time when they asked him about the kingdom of heaven he said, 'The kingdom of heaven is like when a person takes the tiniest of all the seeds, a mustard seed. . . . ' " I hold up my finger as if there were a seed on it, and show it to all of the children. "Look, it is so tiny you can't even see it."

After this point in the presentation my eye contact will be with the parable and not the children unless there is some kind of emergency. I won't look up again until the parable is finished. To a certain degree the children and the room disappear. When I enter the parable it is to discover something for my own life as well as to teach the art of how to do it.

"The kingdom of heaven is like when a person takes the tiniest of all the seeds, a mustard seed, and plants it in the ground." I take the finger with the imaginary seed on it and firmly push it down into the metaphorical soil of the underlay. I hold it there many seconds for the "planting" to take hold.

"And the tiny seed . . . " I begin to unroll the felt tree. I roll it out slowly all the way to the top and then without hurrying unfold the branches from the center outward. The tree shakes out its own shape in the silence and expectation. I then say one word very slowly, "g-r-o-w-s," as the tree is smoothed out.

"It grows into a shrub so big it is like a tree. And . . . "

I reach into the gold parable box and take out a small gold box. I hold it up and show it to the children without speaking. Mysteriously I take off the lid. Inside are birds and nests, enough for all the children. The words are left hanging in the air.

I put down two birds flying toward the tree. "And the birds of the air come and . . . " I put a nest in the tree, and two birds in the nest. "And make their nests there."

Silence. I continue to hold the little gold box. "Look, there are enough birds and nests in here for all of you to put one down where it is best for you. I am going to pass it around this way." I show the way by a movement of the box around the circle from my right to my left.

"There are plenty of birds and nests for everyone. You don't need to hurry. Take your time. We can all be patient. It's fun to see where your birds and nests will be. Here, Billy, we'll begin with you."

It's not always possible to pass around the little box, but today the children seem very settled. I love to do it when I can. Here we go.

The children stay settled, even Robbie. At my left I begin to sense movement. "No, Robbie. You are doing a good job. Stay ready." I touch his knee. "That's the way. You know how to do this. I know it's hard sometimes." My voice becomes softer as I speak to him. It is always hard for Robbie. I suddenly realize how much I really like him and respect his effort to be patient. It *is* hard for him.

The children put the birds and the nests on and around the tree and pass the box to the next child. Some put the nests up high in the branches, and some put them down low. Some even put the nests on the ground. The nests have one, two, or three birds in them.

The children continue to watch, wait, and respect the placing on the objects on the tree and underlay. I wonder what they are thinking. Perhaps they are not thinking anything with their conscious minds. Perhaps they are thinking with their hands. One child puts a bird on the head of the cardboard figure. You can guess who.

The passing of the box around the circle is finally complete. I relax. A wonderful feeling flows through me that Robbie and Billy both made it through on their own without disrupting the circle. With a smile at each one and then at all the children, I say, "This is really good work."

I lean back and take a deep breath, and the smile breaks out again. My leaning back is a shifting of gears that signals to the children that we are about to begin wondering about the parable together out loud.

THE RESPONSE OF WONDERING TOGETHER

"I wonder what this could really be." With my finger I touch the green tree in the middle of the yellow underlay. I move my finger from the base of the tree up to the top and then toward the branches. As I trace the tree's outline, I say again, more slowly, "I wonder what the tree could really be. I wonder if the tree has a name?"

"It's a tree," Dan says.

"It's only a piece of green stuff," Sally murmurs, shrugging her shoulders.

"It is, but it is also more. I wonder what more it could be?"

"It's a place for the birds," Nancy says seriously.

"Hmmm. It could be." My voice balances affirmation and wonder.

Billy suddenly and stridently says, "B-o-r-i-n-g. I've already had this lesson!"

Thank you, Billy, I say to myself. This is the moment I've been waiting for. My open hand goes out, palm down, to signal him to settle down again.

"I know, you've had this lesson before, Billy. Think how many times I've worked with the Parable of the Mustard Seed. Who knows how many times? I still love the parable, and there are still new things waiting for me whenever I go into it again to see.

"Should you stop having Christmas just because you had it last year?" The children shake their heads no. "There's always something new in Christmas. You get new presents. *You* are even new, because you are more grown up than the year before. There are new things in the world each Christmas. The parables are the same way. We do them over and over again because there is always something new to be found there if we have the eyes to see and the ears to hear. If we know how to get ready, we can go inside them to find out."

I really mean that. Today I, too, have discovered something new. Until now I had never thought about the whole parable taking place inside the seed. My whole life is inside a seed that is going to grow to become something that spreads out above with branches, and below with roots. There are so many people from the past who nourish me. So many others will come and settle in my branches and build nests there. There will be grandchildren, if it may be, and great-grandchildren I may never even see. Perhaps these children too are the birds, and their children as well.

I turn my attention back to the parable and the children. "I wonder what this could really be?" I point to the nests for the birds. "I wonder if the birds are happy when they build or find their nests? I wonder if the birds have names? In wonder if the nests have names?"

The children begin to respond to the wondering with their eyes and their bodies. They lean in. Their eyes sparkle. Some carry on an inner dialogue without words; others play with words within their own silent conversation. Other speak out loud.

"That bird's name is Nancy."

"That one is Mommy." Other children say other names.

As they speak, I keep the wondering alive by suggesting new entry points. "I wonder if the person who put the seed in the ground has a name?"

We continue wondering what each part of the parable could really be until the process begins to lose its energy. The children's imaginations grow weary, and the wonder begins to fade. Hopefully, it is just before that moment that I say, "Let's get ready to get out our work now.

"I will go around the circle this way." I sweep my hand from right to left, counterclockwise.

"But can't we go the other way today? I have to wait so long every time," Robbie says.

"We never do. We always go this way, Robbie." I move my hand counterclockwise again. "That's okay. You can be patient. I know you can do it. Don't wait for me to tell you. You can tell yourself, now."

THE PLAY AND ART RESPONSES

"Billy," I say to the first child on my right, "what work would you like to get out today? You can work with today's lesson or choose another lesson you've already had. If there is something you want to work with that you have not had a lesson on, you can always get someone to show you. I will show you, or one of the other children who has had the lesson can show you.

"Would you like to make something about how this parable feels to you? You can use the paints or the clay or the other things on the art shelves. Maybe you'd like to work on something you started another day? We still have the rainbow you started another time if you want to finish that."

"I want to do something with the paints."

"What would you like to make?"

"I don't know."

"Would you like to use the big paints (tempera with big brushes) or the little paints (watercolors)?"

"The big paints."

"What would you like to make? Is it about the lesson today or another lesson?"

"I don't know."

"Do you almost know? Maybe your fingers know. That will be good work, Billy. You need a rug first, then your painting tray. Mrs. Berryman will help you get started if you need help." Billy leaves to get out his work.

"Lucy, what work would you like to get out?" The process continues around the circle. Each child who can make a choice gets up and goes to get out his or her work. Thea helps guide their use of the art materials and helps them work out sharing problems when more than one child wants to use the intentionally limited number of supplies. It is at these moments that ethics is shown, whatever the spoken lesson of the day might be.

I sit there watching the whole complex network of relationships develop around the room as I finish up the circle. I have now gone around the circle twice, helping children try to choose their work. There are still three children left who don't know what to do.

"Do you see this parable? Watch while I put everything away very carefully. I will then bring you another parable from the shelves. We can work on it together right here in our new little circle."

As I go to put away the parable and get another one, I look around the room. Some children are painting. Others are working with clay. Still others are working with wire, wood scraps, or cloth pieces. Thea quietly moves in and out of where a problem presents itself. I return to the three children.

Some children are working directly with other materials. Nancy is working with the Noah material. Phil has spread out the long underlay for the lesson about the Creation. Jim is working with the Advent lesson. Suddenly, I realize that the time is racing to a close.

For the first time I get unsettled. I hate to cut the work period short when the children are so involved. If I suddenly pull them out of their deep concentration, it will burn them. They won't want to go that deep again. They will sense that my time-keeping is more important than their work. What can I do?

Okay, settle down. We have the feast to prepare and enjoy. We have our dismissal to enjoy, as the children leave one by one. I must choose. We can't do both. Feast first . . . We'll do the best we can with the dismissal. The second parable is finished.

I get up and go the doorway. The door is still closed, retaining the integrity of the classroom. I turn off the light. "Listen. I need to speak to everyone at once. Look. Let me see your eyes." I am speaking slowly and softly. "Shhh. Listen to my voice. You need to put your work away. You don't have to be in a hurry, but you need to put it away now.

"If you aren't finished, that's okay. We don't lose children's work here. We will keep it for you to finish even if you can't come back next week. We like your work and want you to have it here when you can come."

As the children begin to put away their work, I notice that Thea has picked three children to help with the feast. I suddenly realize that I didn't finish what I had to say or turn the light back on. I go back to the doorway and stand by the light switch.

"Listen. Let me see your eyes again. Stop what you are doing one more time. When you put your work away, come to the circle. It's time to get ready for our feast. Jill, Dan, and Nancy are going to help today. They are already getting ready, so put your work away now." I turn the light back on.

The children put the lesson materials back on the shelves. The art supplies are put back. Wet paintings are left in the painting trays to dry. I go and sit down in the circle to anchor it and to model what I have just said. As I watch the children winding up their work, I remember that I didn't get to listen to a single child today tell about his or her art response. I make a mental note that we will need a "work day" soon when there is no lesson. The children can finish up some of the projects they have started. I will get to listen to what they have to say about their work then.

THE FEAST

The children are sitting down in the circle. Some settle into the cross-legged, getting-ready position and put their hands on their legs. Others need a look from me to remind them to get ready. I lift up my folded hands and remind a child across the circle to fold his hands.

I begin to think about the lesson and the feast. I suppose some people would want to have the lesson and response at all costs. My tendency is to be sure we have time for the feast.

The children who are helpers are busily setting the table. The "table" is the floor. We even sit on this table, I think. That makes the whole classroom an altar. Napkins are placed in front of each child who is ready. Finally, all are ready and all the napkins are set.

"Remember to unfold your napkin like an underlay. You can open it up like this. It makes a little table." Cookies are placed on the napkins by another one of the helpers. Apple juice is brought to the circle in little cups and placed on the napkins. A new child can't resist picking up his cookie for a taste.

"Remember that we wait until everyone is served. It's more fun to have a feast all together."

"This isn't a feast," blurts out another child who comes infrequently. "It's just juice and cookies."

"Oh, no." I pause. "There's a big difference between a feast and snack. You might have the same food to eat, but that is not what counts. What is important is how you feel about it. Sometimes the food is little but the feelings are big. It's the big feelings that make a feast."

All are served. "Let's say our prayers. If you want to say a prayer today, you may. I will go around the circle and look at you one by one. If you want to say a prayer, go ahead. If you don't feel like it today, then just shake your head no.

"Sometimes prayers are said out loud, and sometimes they are so quiet and inside that only God can hear. You can say them either way. Sometimes prayers don't even have words. They are just being quiet inside or having feelings. You can pray the way you like, but you always need to say 'Amen' out loud so we will know when you are finished."

I begin to go around the circle, looking at each child. Some of the children shake their heads no, and I move on. Most pray silently. Some pray out loud prayers they have learned, and others use their own words. Occasionally, someone sings a prayer. When we complete the circle it is my turn.

"I would like to say a prayer." I fold my hands, close my eyes, and bow my head, just as the children have done.

"Thank you, God, for these wonderful children and for our feast. Amen." I say each word slowly, dwelling inside the world each one makes. I say the words not so much as words but as experiences, experiences that fill me up to overflowing.

Some of the children laugh. "You always say that," they say.

"I know. It is what I really mean. It is what I feel. That's what a prayer is. It's when you try to say to God what is most true." Maybe the honesty of the prayer makes them nervous or uneasy. Perhaps it makes them happy but they want to test whether or not I mean those words so much. Oh, well, maybe they just want to take over the circle again. Children. People.

I notice Thea is pointing at her watch. She is opening the door a little and talking to some of the parents outside. They have come for their children. Some are in a hurry to go home. Others are in a hurry to get to church. They are anxious, and although they wouldn't think so, they are loud. I begin to feel anxious again and then I settle down.

"When you are finished—and we need to finish up now— put your napkins in your cup, and put your cup in the wastebasket. Then come back to the circle, so we can say good-bye."

SAYING GOOD-BYE

The children move back and forth. The circle is unsettled. I'm not handling this too well. "Come sit down, now. We need to say good-bye. Your parents are here."

The children are still restless. Thea is ready to call the names one by one so each child can come up and say good-bye in a relaxed way. I love this. It is like a blessing. I love to tell them that they are good children and that they did good work. I love to hold them by the hands and ask each one how he or she got to be so wonderful.

Billy jumps up. He just caught sight of his dad. "I've got to go."

"I know, Billy. Good-bye. Tell Mrs. Berryman good-bye as you go out the door."

The other children come up in little clusters. The room is suddenly empty. I wave to Thea as I head out the door behind the children to hurry to the eleven o'clock liturgy.

With younger children I am usually much more precise than with older ones. I use an even greater economy of words. With older children there is more talking and playful banter back and forth. It is as if the children of late childhood want to play at three levels. There is the lesson. The lesson is important, and even if the children do not appear to focus as deeply as the little ones, there is still a lot of concentration. Second, there is the game going on about whether they will attend to the lesson. They can play this game while still being in the lesson. The third level is the game where both you and the children know about the other two levels, so from time to time you and the children comment on that to let one another know all three games are in process.

I occasionally miss something or don't get everything done smoothly, as I would like to. This was illustrated by the ending narrated here. All in all, however, the approach described in this chapter seems to be so tuned to children's needs and to the spirit of religious language that it runs very well anyway when properly set up. Something must be right. The children seem to be so deeply happy. I know I am. Thea is, too.

If the children are deeply happy, then there must be some need they have that is being satisfied. What could that be? We need to ask the children, but that is difficult. Children cannot provide us with an analysis of their own thinking. They are not mature enough, and self-analysis is complicated in itself. The next chapter describes one way to "ask the children," and it tells how they have answered.

3 Children at Play

Howard Gardner[1] has proposed that human beings have special kinds of intelligences, such as linguistic, musical, logical-mathematical, spatial, and bodily-kinesthetic ones. He further proposed that special kinds of teaching are needed for the learning of these special ways of communicating. I would like to suggest that theological cognition is a "frame of meaning" that can be identified in addition to the ones Gardner has noted. We need a special way of teaching to best develop the power of this type of cognition for the work that God created it to do.

To suggest what this special way of teaching is, I will present a study of two boys I will call Bobby and Jimmy. The study covers their responses to the Parable of the Mustard Seed in a research class. The responses occurred during eight Saturdays of a twelve-week period in the fall of 1981. Bobby was six years old and Jimmy was seven.

The series of pictures produced by Bobby and Jimmy crystallized my thinking about the function of religious language in child development and confirmed the religious education approach that this book presents. More than any other event, this series of children's responses also committed me to continue to follow the winding track of this project wherever it might lead.

THE ORIGIN OF THE RESEARCH

As related in the last chapter, the dream of the project was initiated while I was a student in Bergamo, Italy, at the Center for

Advanced Montessori Studies, where I met Sofia Cavalletti. She not only inspired me to begin this work but gave me the conceptual tools, the practical guidance, and the encouragement to start.

The dream of a research project became a reality in Houston in 1975, when I was director of Christian education at St. John's Presbyterian Church. We used this approach in our church school for children (1975–1977). We also used it at Pines Presbyterian Church when I was director of Christian education there (1977–1980). It was at Pines that the first class for adolescents was held. The first class for adults was held at Church of the Redeemer in Houston around 1980, where several children's classes were also conducted.

It took three years (1975–1978) to construct and learn how to use the materials, method, and environment adequately to begin to do research. A special Saturday morning research class was begun at Pines in 1978.

In 1979 the research moved to the Institute of Religion in the Texas Medical Center, where I soon focused on the work with children. It was especially during the years 1979–1985 that I enjoyed the stimulation and support of many child psychiatrists, child life workers, physicians, social workers, psychologists, and pastoral care people in the Texas Medical Center.

We began on the second floor of the Institute of Religion building, but the next year we moved downstairs into a splendid facility across from my office. The fine observation room gave parents and researchers the opportunity to watch the classes in process. Thea and I continued to be the primary investigators and teachers. The results of the research at this time were used to develop an approach to the pastoral care of children in hospitals, but I continued to consult and work in churches in the field of religious education.

Ultimately the Children's Center project moved with me to Christ Church Cathedral, where the research has continued. Now the major effort of the project is to deepen and broaden this approach to the needs of religious education in the parish.

Eight classes are now using this approach at the cathedral. The classes involve more than two hundred children from two through twelve years of age and about twenty-four volunteer teachers, equally divided between men and women. Several national workshops including observations of children are done there each year.

THE RESEARCH SETTING

The families of the research group came from a variety of socio-economic, religious, and school settings in Houston. They found their way to us by word of mouth. When Bobby and Jimmy were attending the original Children's Center in the fall of 1981, the group included about twelve children from ages three through ten. The group expanded during that fall term into two groups, two through seven and seven through twelve years of age. The next year classes expanded again until a ceiling was set at about twenty children in each group.

About half of the children came from Montessori schools during this period. This seemed relevant at the time, since the approach to classroom management in the Children's Center draws heavily on the method of Maria Montessori.[2] Since that time, however, our abbreviated Montessori model has been shown to work well without Montessori-trained children, both in our research group and when used by volunteers who are not professional teachers.

The space and time for our Godly play experience were described in the last chapter. The children are surrounded by parables, sacred stories, and liturgical symbols of the Christian language system when they enter the room. The images of this language system have been made into objects the children can manipulate.

At the beginning of the class the children are invited into a circle for a lesson. After the lesson they are invited to "get out their work." They can choose lessons to work on from the shelves, or they can make an art response to the lesson of the day. Constructive wandering is also supported (note Bobby on the fifth Saturday in the upcoming account).

The "material" that Bobby and Jimmy found so useful and interesting, the Parable of the Mustard Seed, was presented in the way described in chapter 2. When the shrub "grows," a green felt "tree"[3] is unrolled. After the teacher and children place birds and nests around it, they wonder together about what the parable might "really be." The children are then excused one at a time from the circle and can choose their first bit of work, which may or may not be related overtly to the lesson.

The research classes are two hours long. The lesson and wondering with the teacher take about thirty minutes, and the work period about sixty minutes. The final thirty minutes are devoted to putting away things, gathering again in the circle, getting ready for the feast, saying our prayers, sharing the feast, and saying good-bye. This two-hour period is a great luxury when compared to many church school settings that have only a "forty-five–minute hour" or less to work with.

The structure of classroom time is shaped by the deep structure of the Holy Eucharist. There is first an approach through the Liturgy of the Word: (1) a Greeting, (2) the Lesson, and (3) a Response. We then continue with the Liturgy of Holy Communion, which includes (4) Setting the Table, (5) Sharing the Feast, (6) the Blessing, and (7) the Dismissal.

The reason for using the deep structure of Holy Eucharist as the pattern for the class is that the language of religion—a language system people can learn and choose to use like any other linguistic domain, such as science, ethics, art, or law—is grounded in a special kind of experience. This experience is the relationship with God in community. This way of communicating we call "worship" has taken the classical shape of the Eucharist for nearly two thousand years.

The theological control for this research is the conscious attempt to steer between blasphemy (thinking that I know in advance, as if I were God, what the children can and will do in this situation) and idolatry (turning religious language into an object of worship in itself rather than seeing it as a tool to make meaning and find direction in life and death with God and with one another). The need to carefully steer a path between these two dangers of distortion in the religious journey is as ancient as the religious journey itself.

TWO BOYS AND A PARABLE

Our primary focus in this journey will be on Bobby, but, as you will see, the interaction between the two boys and the difference in their responses to the parable are also of great interest. Our description will move week by week, and then a discussion and some conclusions will follow.

The First Saturday

The lesson on this Saturday was the Parable of the Good Shepherd. Both boys responded with pictures related to it. Bobby made one picture, and Jimmy made two.

The Second Saturday

This day's lesson was the Parable of the Mustard Seed. Bobby made two large paintings with tempera paint and large paint brushes. The first painting had a large, thick vertical shaft, rounded at the top in the middle of the page. On the left side was a large black bird, and above it were two smaller birds. They were pale blue. On the right side of the tree were several other pale blue birds.

I sat down with Bobby and quietly enjoyed the painting. I did not say anything except "Hmm. I like your painting." I then waited. Bobby sat looking at his picture. Eventually he began to tell me about it. The large bird on the left side, he said, was an "eagle flying to get the others." I asked, "How did they feel about the eagle?" He said that they were "happy and sad about the big one." I nodded my head that I understood and took what he was telling me very seriously. Bobby continued, "Coming to get the babies to eat them. . . . " He did not say anything else. We sat there a few minutes more. He then put away his paints and cleaned his paint brushes.

After asking Bobby if I might write on his picture, I made notes in pencil about what he said. I keep notes for the research, but they also help parents see what the child has said so they do not jump to conclusions about what he or she has expressed in the painting.

Jumping to adult conclusions about children's art puts the children in the position of having to choose between being true to their own interpretation of personal experience and being true to what their parents say the experience means. The double bind makes either response painful. It is a choice between identity and nurture, both of which the young child needs. It is unfair to set up a child for such a double bind, but it is also almost impossible not to do so. The only way out of this impasse is through humor and playfulness.

I also asked Bobby if I could keep his painting for a week to take a photograph of it. He said yes, so I was able to make a slide of the picture and keep a record for reference. If he had declined, the picture would have been lost for the research. Taking pictures during the class calls too much attention to the children as research subjects and disrupts the class, so many records have been lost due to this ethical and research problem. I always value the child's needs over my research needs.

The second painting was also tempera and on big paper (12″ X 18″). Like the first, it had a large cylinder in the middle of the paper, but this one had an oval at the bottom of it. Birds were flying on both sides this time. They were a variety of colors now rather than just pale blue.

In the first painting the eagle was the largest figure, but this time it was smaller than most of the other birds. Bobby said, "The birds are many colors now. Here is the eagle [pointing to the figure on the left side of the tree]." He was matter-of-fact about the second painting and kept referring back to the first one as he talked about the second one. He paused and then said, "No stuff happening. All happy. Bited him all up [pointing to the eagle]. Laughing [the birds] at him [the eagle]."

We turn now to Jimmy's first response of this day. In the circle I said, "I wonder where this could really be [sweeping my hand over the whole Parable of the Mustard Seed that was laid out on the floor]?" Jimmy said, "It's in Houston."

This response is ambiguous. It could mean that the parable is *about* Houston, that Houston is "in the parable." It could also mean that we were sitting there around the parable in the classroom, which was in Houston. It was my intuition at the time that Jimmy was "in the parable" and was speaking about Houston being "in the parable" as well.

Jimmy also made a painting response to the Parable of the Mustard Seed. It looked much like the second painting he had

made the week before in response to the Parable of the Good
Shepherd. He continued a sun motif from the week before that
connected the point of emphasis, first the sheepfold and now
the tree, with the sun. On this Saturday, five out of eight children present, including Bobby and Jimmy, responded to the
Parable of the Mustard Seed with a painting about it.

The Third Saturday

On the third Saturday Bobby made another picture of the Parable of the Mustard Seed. The lesson was about the seven days
of creation. When it came time for Bobby to get out his work,
however, he chose the Parable of the Mustard Seed. He took the
gold box from the shelf and presented the parable to himself.
He then made an art response in tempera on the large paper.

In the center of this painting was another large cylinder.
There were little birds all over the top of the tree, which was
larger than the shaft of the trunk. More tiny birds were flying
toward the tree from the left side of the paper. At ground level, represented by a line, stood a man. Another line went from
a gun the man was holding up to a bird flying toward the tree.
Red dashes fell down to the base of the tree into a container.
Not all of this was obvious until Bobby and I began to visit together about the painting.

"I like your painting," I said, and then waited. Finally I
touched a bird gently with my finger. "The bird got shot,"
Bobby said. He pointed to the figure on the ground and said,
"Man with gun." His finger traced the red dashes down to the
container, and he said, "Blood dropping down into nest."

Another dimension was introduced as Bobby went on.
"Other page [picture] don't have names [for the birds]. These
do. All are coming to nests." Bobby went on. "It's like Jimmy's.
He was going to write [paint] a lot of birds. My tree is bigger."
He had been watching Jimmy as he worked and even looked
over at Jimmy's picture as he spoke to me.

The same Saturday Jimmy first made a painting about "the
sixth day" (of creation). The painting continued his theme of
the sun linking to the primary focus in the picture. The second

picture Jimmy made was a tree related to the Parable of the Mustard Seed. His primary comment was that the birds could all fit into the nests because the birds were small and the nests were large. This picture, which Bobby had watched him make, did not look at all like the one Bobby made. It looked much more like a tree than Bobby's did.

The Fourth Saturday

The lesson this day was the circle of the liturgical year. Despite the lesson of the day, Jimmy and Bobby worked together again on the Parable of the Mustard Seed. Both made pencil drawings of the tree. Unfortunately, the originals were both lost, so I do not have slides of them. They did not comment on their pictures.

The Fifth Saturday

On this Saturday the lesson was the Parable of the Pearl. Bobby was unable to choose a piece of work and concentrate on it. I finally asked him to walk slowly around the room and look on all the shelves to see if anything called to him for his work. Bobby wandered, looked on the shelves, and watched other children work. He visited quietly with the other children as well. He did not make an art or play response that day.

Jimmy's day was quite different from Bobby's. He made a response to the lesson. As he was telling me about his painting, he said, "These little things are the parables. No, they are the pearls."

At the end of each class the children return to the circle and get ready for the feast. They take turns serving. The helpers place napkins in front of the children and then put bread, cheese, apples, or other healthful and festive things on the napkins. Juice is also set out in little cups. We say our prayers and then share the feast together. The children are each invited to pray, but there is no pressure put on them to do so. Many of the children signal that they "pass" by shaking their heads or saying no.

I tell the children that there are all kinds of prayers. Some prayers are made with their own words, like regular talking. There are also prayers that use other people's words that they remember and say. There are long prayers and short prayers. Sometimes prayers don't have any words at all. They are feelings. Prayers can be said out loud or quietly "inside." God can feel and know all kinds of prayers, however they are prayed.

The handling of the prayers is important to briefly mention now because Bobby continued to shake his head no. Jimmy on the other hand, always indicated his desire to say a prayer. His manner of prayer was to pray intently but silently.

The Sixth Saturday

The lesson this Saturday was the Parable of the Good Samaritan. Bobby did not want to get any work out. When this happens in the circle, the child remains sitting so he or she can have more time to choose. When we go around the circle, the children who choose work leave one by one. We then go around again until all have been able to get up and move with intention to some task.

Bobby stayed in the circle a long time this day. Finally, he got up and made an art response. It was a response to the Parable of the Good Samaritan, the lesson for the day. He made almost no comment about it at all.

Jimmy made three pictures this Saturday. The first and second ones were about the Good Samaritan. His pictures focused on the violence of the parable. He said, "They jumped out on that guy" and "The guy got hurt." The third picture he made was about the Parable of the Good Shepherd, the lesson of the first week, now forty-two days ago.

The Seventh Saturday

Noah and the Flood was the lesson on the seventh Saturday. Bobby made no response to it or anything else. He wandered. Jimmy made four pictures. The first two were about Noah and the Flood. The third one was about the Parable of the Good Shepherd. The last one was about the Parable of the Mustard

Seed. Jimmy made the first with ink markers, the second with tempera paint, the third with markers, and the last with a pencil. I asked him, "Where is the mustard seed?" He said, "It is the tree."

At the feast Jimmy again said a silent prayer. I am the last one in the circle to decide about praying, and I usually pray the same prayer out loud. I say, "Thank you, God, for these wonderful children and for our feast." On this day, when I finished by saying "Amen," Jimmy spoke up and said, "That's what I said, same as Mr. Berryman." Again, Bobby did not say a prayer.

The Eighth Saturday

I had to be away to attend a professional meeting in Canada. The children did not come to the Children's Center for class.

The Ninth Saturday

This day the lesson was about Advent, which began the next day. The Advent lesson first presents the Holy Family. The wooden figures are on top of the main shelf in the classroom. They sit on a cloth that is the color of the liturgical season. A small circular tray is set on the presentation rug in the circle, and each person and animal is named and valued as it is placed upon it. The cloth is changed to the color of the new season, and then each piece is carefully replaced on the new color.

Additional lessons about Advent use a set of cards with symbols for the prophets, the Holy Family, the shepherds, and the Magi. This will be mentioned in some detail, because of the impact it seemed to have on Bobby.

An abstract cardboard replica of Bethlehem is placed in the center of the circle of children. The words that are said and the way the lesson is laid out suggest that we are all on the way to Bethlehem with the Holy Family during Advent. A new card is laid out each week, and a large purple or rose candle is placed by the card. The candle is lighted and in turn we enjoy the light of the prophets, the Holy Family, the shepherds, and the Magi. The final card laid down is white. The white Christ Candle from the Baptism lesson is placed by it. The candle is for the Christ Child and the mystery of Christmas.

On this day when the shepherds were being placed on the wooden tray at the very beginning of the series of lessons, one of them fell over. Bobby said, "Looks like that shepherd's dead." He grew agitated. I set it upright. Bobby smiled and relaxed again.

On this day Bobby made three art responses. The first was in crayon on a small piece of paper, 9" X 6". It was the most tree-looking tree Bobby had yet made. It was the first one with branches, and they were green! It also looked rooted in the yellow ground. Bobby wrote his name along the contour of the earth. Blue birds were flying away from the tree to the right. On the top of the tree was a half circle in which sat a bird a little bigger than the others. It seemed to be nesting and was more formed than the rest. It was yellow.

I sat quietly beside Bobby and waited for him to speak. I showed how much I liked his work and how important I thought it was by touching it with care. I decided not to touch any specific figure in the picture.

I waited. Finally, Bobby said, "The mustard tree." I shook my head yes. He continued, "These are flying away [the birds on the right]. They are going to get some food for the baby." He pointed to a little speck on a branch at the lower left of the tree's branches. He said, "A little . . . " Pointing to the right side of the lower branches, he said, "A new bird." He brought his finger up to the top of the tree and pointed to the yellow bird nesting there. He said more firmly, "A new bird."

The second picture Bobby made on the ninth Saturday was about the Parable of the Good Shepherd. The sheepfold is in the upper middle of the picture, with black rocks on the lower left and a blue pond on the lower right. One figure he called "the Good Shepherd" and what appears to be another figure, which he did not identify, are standing in the middle of an open gate. There is one sheep inside the sheepfold. There are no other sheep in the painting.

Bobby said, "The Good Shepherd." I nodded. He pointed to the figure in the gate and said, "He's letting the sheep out." He paused and then said, "There's just one."

The third picture Bobby made was on the smallest paper (9″ X 6″). It was in chalk. He worked very rapidly and came over to me in a decisive way. Birds were flying away in all directions from another naturalistic tree. Even the yellow bird had taken flight. He merely put the picture down and walked away without comment.

This Saturday Jimmy made four pictures. The first one was about the Advent lesson. He told me that Jesus was in "his bed." The picture showed a candle and a wreath. The second picture was about "the parable of the guy who's half-dead [the Good Samaritan]." The third picture was about the Parable of the Pearl. The fourth picture was a small pencil drawing of the Parable of the Mustard Seed. Jimmy's only comment was to say "The Parable of the Mustard Seed."

During the feast that day, Bobby shook his head yes for the first time when it was his turn to choose to pray. He prayed silently. Jimmy also prayed, as he did every Saturday that term. *This turned out to be the only time Bobby prayed during the whole twelve weeks.*

The Tenth Saturday

The lesson on this day was about the second week of Advent. The card for the prophets pointing the way was laid down again, followed by the card for the Holy Family. The wooden figures were placed upon the Holy Family card. The candles were lighted, and we enjoyed the light of the prophets and the Holy Family as they (and we) made our way toward Bethlehem.

Bobby made his final Mustard Seed picture that day. It was a small pencil drawing. The tree in it shifted back toward being somewhat non-naturalistic again. The two sides of the trunk in the center of the page swept up in concave curves from each side, and a ball sat on the top. Three birds flew away to the right from the trunk. I sat quietly.

Bobby seemed ready to sit a long time with me without speaking. Finally, I said, "Where is the bad bird?" He did not respond. I tried again. "You know, the one that was hurting the other birds." Bobby said, "He's gone." He then sighed a deep sigh. "All the others are asleep."

Jimmy did three pictures on that day. The first one was related to the presentation. He made a picture of Bethlehem and a path going toward it. The second picture was about the Parable of the Pearl. The third picture was the Parable of the Mustard Seed. I sat down beside him to appreciate his work. We sat there for some time, and then I asked, "Are the birds coming or going?" He said, "Coming."

The Eleventh Saturday

Bobby was away traveling with his family for the Christmas holidays. Jimmy made six pictures, all related to the Advent lessons. They were of candles, wreaths, prophets, and Bethlehem.

The Twelfth Saturday

Both boys were away with their families for the Christmas holidays.

DISCUSSION

Some General Observations

The first point of interest is that Bobby usually produced pictures related to the Parable of the Mustard Seed on days when Jimmy did (classes two, three, four, nine, and ten). There was one exception (class seven), and it was on one of Bobby's wandering days (classes five, six, and seven). This suggests the powerful influence and importance of community when children are learning how to use religious language. The two boys helped each other sustain their interest in this parable, and the independent work of all the children and the teachers gave them permission to continue to follow what seemed important to them.

Second, it is important to note that the juxtapositions between the parable and other lessons had an influence on the boys' work with the parable. For Bobby, the lesson about Advent on day nine seem to have linked the images of birth and new life and reframed the "eating of babies" by the eagle when the series began. Bobby said that the birds in his first picture of day nine were flying away, "going to get some food for the baby." This was also the day when Bobby's trees became more naturalistic and the image of the "new bird" was introduced. The idea for "food for their babies" also came up in an aside related to Bobby's last picture on day ten.

What this suggests is the importance of having the whole context of religious language present in the room, as it is in church worship. The architecture, the lections of the church year, and the continuity of Holy Communion in the classical Eucharist provide the possibility of juxtapositions that nudge the creative process into action.

The whole series of eight pictures for Bobby and five pictures for Jimmy, about the Parable of the Mustard Seed, done over a period of eight weeks, suggests the importance of being able to return again and again to an image that has special significance for the individual. This means that in teaching the art of using religious language such an opportunity needs to be given and supported by allowing the children to choose their work whatever the daily lesson is.

When we look at the pictures of the two boys side by side, we see how different they are despite the boys' interaction with each other and the use of the same image to make meaning. Many of Bobby's responses—eating the babies and "biting" the eagle on day two, the hunter's shot and dripping blood on day three, and the death concern about the shepherd on day nine—suggest that Bobby was attempting to cope with the existential issue of death. Even the tree itself seems to signal something ominous and dangerous, such as death and separation, until it turns into a more naturalistic tree and becomes a place of nourishment.

Jimmy seems to have felt that the tree was a place of nourishment all through the series of his pictures. At the end he decided to stay flying toward the tree, while Bobby decided that he could fly away from it to new existential issues such as freedom now that the "bad bird is gone" (day ten).

Bobby connected his use of the parable with the pattern of the creative process. This is natural for human beings when they are allowed to do so and can find a safe place in which to create new ideas or new frames of reference. He used this process in many of his responses to the lessons and existential issue they connected with, but he also used it in a more over-arching way that encompassed many weeks.

The creative process has been widely studied (please see chapter 6) and has been applied explicitly to pastoral care and counseling and implicitly to religious education by James E. Loder in *The Transforming Moment*.[4] What is agreed on in this literature is that the process has a regular pattern of about five steps. Much more will be said about this in the sixth chapter.

The first step in my view of the pattern is a disruption of one's circle of meaning. Bobby's disruption of meaning was ex-pressed in the early pictures of the threatening tree and the dangerous eagle. Jimmy did not seem to experience such a dis-ruption. His circle of meaning seemed to remain complete during the whole series, and his tree remained a source of nourishment and "nesting."

The second step in the creative process is the scanning for a new frame of meaning to cope with the disruption. The scan-ning began at once for Bobby on day two with his second pic-ture and continued to the ninth Saturday, when the lessons on Advent began.

The third step is insight. The energy used for scanning is converted into energy to create the new frame of meaning. On both day nine and day ten Bobby worked out this solution in terms of nourishment and the ability to fly away to new things despite the danger and threat of death and separation in life.

The fourth step in the pattern of the creative process is the articulation of the new way to tie meaning back together and thus satisfy one's religious need (Latin *re* + *ligare*, to bind back together).

The fifth step in the pattern is the testing of the newly ar-ticulated discovery against the experience of other persons, and deciding. Bobby brought his concluding piece of art to me to say he was finished. He was ready to move on.

The Existential Ground for the Process

If the art of using religious language is learned while creating with it, and if it functions to help one cope with one's existential limits, as in the case of Bobby, then a pattern is revealed that stimulates the creative process at all levels of human functioning—biological, psychological, social, and spiritual. What is happening is not just problem solving about the natural world. It is the raising of awareness that creating is a whole new way of being in the world, the way of being in the image of God, the Creator. When this experience is supported as it was for Bobby, even the threat of death and separation can be reframed so that one can "fly away" to take up new challenges.

Existential issues are issues that do not yield to therapy. Awareness of such issues is not a symptom of pathology. It is a symptom that one is a human being. Pathology begins when so much energy is used to deny existential limits that energy is no longer available for growth. The major existential issues are death, the threat of freedom, aloneness, and the need for meaning.[5]

The Focus of This Study and Its Evaluation

Each way of exploring human experience has its own methodology and leads to its own set of issues and discoveries. If we focus our attention on the biological issues of human interaction, then we might discuss such things as how Bobby's pictures are "really" about an intuited biological threat such as cancer. Such a biological discussion presumes certain rules of observation, a technology for investigation, and a particular way of drawing conclusions about Bobby's biological health. Bobby had nothing like this lurking in the background of his paintings, I am happy to say. The biology of Bobby's life remains in the background.

Psychological issues are also important and can be uncovered through art and play. These issues also remain in the background for this study. If we were to look at psychological issues in Bobby's life, an interesting one might be how Bobby's new male teacher, myself, might be a phallic threat to his development. This discussion, too, would have its own rules of observation, way of investigation, and formalities for drawing conclusions about what Bobby's pictures "really" mean from this point of view.

Social issues also remain in the background for this study. If we were to focus on social issues in Bobby's life, we might want to discuss the fact that at school during this period he was worried about the threats of a schoolyard bully. (This information came from Bobby's parents.) We might further want to compare Bobby's experience in school with Jimmy's. This discussion, too, would have its own rules of observation and discourse for deciding what Bobby's pictures "really" mean in social terms.

When we choose to look at Bobby's theological world, we also stipulate a set of criteria for our observations and evaluation. We leave behind biological, psychological, and social language worlds and their rules for study and turn to what is appropriate for theological cognition. What concerns us in this study is the language of existential issues and how Bobby's experience of limit was expressed within the system of Christian religious language.

Bobby, the community of children, and I played together in a game of ultimate concern. Bobby was given permission not only verbally but also nonverbally to work on existential issues with this special language. We might say, then, that what was going on was the careful study of the many factors involved in a case of spiritual direction. It was not a controlled scientific experiment to show whether a particular method of education does or does not work. By definition, studies of theological cognition cannot be controlled in the way that studies about knowledge of the natural world can be controlled. This distinction involves more than different languages and criteria for investigation. In theological cognition God is the ultimate variable.

A theological interpretation of what was happening during the creation of this series of pictures is that both boys seemed to be seeking coherence in the largest possible terms when they meditated again and again on the Parable of the Mustard Seed. Their sensorimotor knowing and art expression engaged their theological "frame of mind" in a powerful and specific way to stimulate its growth while using it to make meaning.

The two boys did not make adult distinctions or think about their thinking as older children and adults might do. On the other hand, we adults would be hard pressed to say what they discovered by this kind of theological cognition better than they said it with their pictures. We adults talk "about" such things more conceptually and with greater differentiation and abstraction than children can. It may be that these adult abilities are not an improvement but a disability when it comes to coping with existential issues.

The ability to talk *about* existential issues turns personal experiences into abstractions. The abstractions tend to mask the existential issues by intellectualizing them. Such an effort to keep conceptual control over existential issues ultimately is doomed, for we are *not* in ultimate control.

Bobby struggled primarily with death as separation and extinction. He then shifted to coping with the threat of freedom. Jimmy continued to seek nourishment in the safety of the status quo. Perhaps Jimmy, too, will become ready to take a risk and continue to grow. Perhaps a crisis will present itself so that he will have to grow or be trapped in a defensive retreat from the threat of freedom.

There is a risk at any stage of development, since a person who finally realizes that he or she is really free also has to take responsibility for his or her choices and actions. To put this issue of existential freedom in the language of the boys: Jimmy flies back to the tree, while Bobby flies away a "new bird."

It is very Christian to speak of Bobby's "new birth" and his "turning." It is a turning that responds to the Creator and creates a new view of life that transcends the existential box he found himself in but had no words for until he found the Parable of the Mustard Seed.

CONCLUSION

If Bobby and Jimmy had only been allowed to work with the lesson of the day, or if they had not been allowed to work with each other, there would have been no series of pictures and insights such as the ones I have described. If other lessons such as the Advent lesson had not been presented, and if the whole environment had not been available to Bobby for constructive choosing, wandering, and scanning, has "turning" might not have taken place.

This study suggests some conclusions about what we need as objectives to guide Christian education when its goal is defined as teaching the art of theological cognition by means of religious language. There are six such objectives:

1. Children need to learn how to wonder in religious education so they can "enter" religious language rather than merely repeat it or talk about it.

2. Children need to be able to work together in a religious education classroom to support and respect one another and one another's work. Teachers need to help shape such a community around the values of respect and love.

3. Children need to be able to choose their work in the classroom so they can return again and again to images that "work" for them to help them cope with their existential limits and ultimate concerns.

4. The art of using religious language needs to be learned in an environment filled with the whole system of religious language for sensorimotor learning so that the lessons presented can be in juxtaposition with the issues being worked on and with the whole system of images that foster creative coping with ultimate concerns.

5. Religious language needs to be learned in an environment that gives permission for and supports the connecting of this powerful language, the creative process, and the experience of the Creator.

6. The time of religious education needs to be shaped by the classical structure of the Holy Eucharist to provide the most tested approach to God, the Creator.

The curious thing about religious language, however, is that the primary goal, the child's encounter with God, can be achieved only indirectly. Even if the six objectives are taken care of by the teaching team, the child's encounter with God is a relationship that is beyond the team's control. This curiosity, as well as how the preceding objectives can be accomplished in the classroom, will be explored more deeply and broadly in the next two chapters, which take up the spoken and the unspoken lesson in some detail.

4 The Spoken Lesson

The method of religious education we are exploring uses primarily story telling, but it can't be reduced to story telling. A reduction is easy to spot. People say something like "Oh, it's only story telling." They trim the event or idea to fit into the mental forms they already have in their mind's storeroom. Reduction is the overassimilation of the new into the old. In contrast, accommodation occurs when one's mental structures change to take in what is new, without trimming it, so that it can be understood on its own terms.

Godly play involves a combination of six factors working together to create a situation in which the art of using religious language can be learned well. By the grace of God the learner's deep identity sometimes emerges indirectly from what we might call, following Winnicott's phrase about mothering, "good enough" teaching.

The deep identity Godly play allows to emerge is the image of the Creator. Much more is accomplished by this approach, but its primary organizing image is that of the creature and Creator at play together, creating. The word we human beings use to indicate what creating feels like is "love." In the animal, mineral, and plant kingdoms "creating" might be called something else, but we call it love when it has to do with us in all of our biological, psychological, social, and spiritual dimensions.

The following diagram shows the six factors needed to create this situation of good-enough teaching and suggests the complex network of interconnections among them:

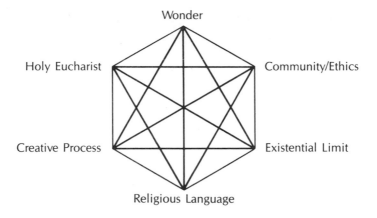

TEACHING TROUGH THE SPOKEN LESSON

I have already said that the presenter of the lesson needs to enter religious language to model how to make meaning with it.
What does the term *modeling* mean in this context? There are
three primary dimensions to this modeling. They can be shown
by one of the triangles in the hexagon model of the method
just presented:

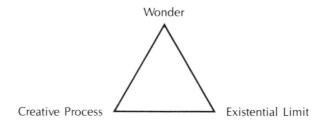

The key to the spoken lesson is the teacher as the storyteller. The goal of the story telling is to engage wonder, the creative process, and the awareness of our existential limits as
human beings in both the speaker and the listener. This is a co-
operative venture between the children and the adult teachers.

When the teacher truly is wondering, the children sense
wonder in the air. It manifests itself in the playfulness present
in the room. Permission and reinforcement are present to en-
courage it. When the teacher enters religious language with

wonder, he or she shows the children by example how to open the creative process.

The storyteller also embodies the creative process in action. The storyteller does this by taking delight in the new insights of the children in their own discoveries about life. In chapter 5 we will talk about how to support the deep pattern of the imagination in Godly play, and in chapter 6 we will discuss the imagination in detail. At this point it is enough to note that the involvement of children and adult teachers with the creative process presents a strange problem.

It is very difficult to keep from sharing a new and significant discovery. Archimedes leapt out of his bath and ran naked into the streets of Syracuse shouting "Eureka!" when he discovered how to determine the purity of gold in Hieron's new crown without melting it down. All he had to do was to see how much water the crown displaced, much as his body displaced water when he lowered it into his bath. Wow! He had to tell everyone immediately. Discoveries spring to life often when you are teaching by the method of Godly play. The problem is that if you, the teacher, tell the children about each new discovery, you take away the child's opportunity to discover such things personally.

Holding back answers is quite different from the usual view of teaching. This point illustrates how the goal of this approach to religious education is not to transfer answers or facts. It is not to teach words as ends in themselves. It is to teach the art of *using* the language to make meaning and find direction in life and death. Like any art, this takes practice and it requires learning by doing.

The worst case of sharing or not sharing discoveries happens when the teacher becomes rigid about *always* telling the children or *never* telling them about a personal discovery. The feelings attached to the rigidity of either kind convey the message that discoveries are uncomfortable to share.

The second-worst case happens when the teacher can't decide when to share or not to share. The anxiety that develops about this indecision teaches the children that discovery makes one anxious. Such a feeling can block the creative process.

The best approach to sharing or not sharing new insights is to balance the risk of taking away the child's chance to make

the discovery with the awareness that showing ourselves happily struck by a new insight reinforces the child's enjoyment of
the creative process. The point is that we should accent helping
the child make discoveries. Sometimes, however, we just can't
help announcing a new insight of our own.

The teacher's attitude toward existential issues is also important. Experiences such as death, the threat of freedom, the
need for meaning, or the unavoidable aloneness that marks us
as human beings often raise the defenses of both adults and
children. Awareness and permission work together to counteract such avoidance. If we are repressing the awareness of existential limits in our own lives, we will communicate that to the
children. Awareness of such limits and permission to deal with
them enable the children to be deeply realistic about who they
are.

There is much more that is communicated with the telling
of the parable or sacred story, or the showing of a liturgical
symbol or action. It is this "much more" that is so important
for this kind of story telling. The significance of telling the stories of the Bible can be highlighted best by comparing telling
and listening with writing and reading.

TELLING AND LISTENING, READING AND WRITING

I write this section with a smile. It is ironic or even downright
funny to be *writing* about the virtues of speaking. It is also
amusing to think that Socrates and Jesus, two of the people
who most profoundly have influenced Western civilization,
wrote nothing.

Socrates was memorialized by the young Plato, who tried
to capture his teacher's special quality of communication by
writing it down in dialogue form. Plato was no romantic, however, when it came to speaking. He banished the poets (*rhap-
sodes*) from his ideal republic as part of his attack against the
oral culture that had developed around the recitation of
Homeric poetry.[1]

Writing down what Jesus said was done by many authors.
Four stories of Jesus were finally selected as the official ones.

All four, but especially Mark's, retain some flavor of the spoken word. Probably, the first element of the tradition to be set down in writing was the passion narrative. The letters of Paul, as well as the letters referred to as "First Peter" and "Hebrews," frequently refer to it. The passion narrative was combined with collections of Jesus' sayings, which had circulated previously in oral form, to fill out the stories.

Paul's letters were written from about A.D. 34–62 on papyrus strips, beaten into whitish, durable sheets. The strips probably were rolled, folded over, tied, and sealed. One letter could make quite a large bundle. The actual writing usually was done by professional writers, the media experts of the day. Writing and receiving a letter were much more dramatic then than they are today. They were media events.

The letters of Paul were circulating during the period when the Gospels still were being written down. By the end of the first century both the letters of Paul and the Gospels were well known as written documents, but when people referred to "the scriptures" they meant the Jewish scriptures. The value of the new writings as scripture was still being weighed.

Paul seems to have been concerned about turning "Christ" into written words. He worried that writing about Christ's words might turn the mystical experience of being "in Christ" into an object. The object, the writing, might even begin to be worshiped in itself. He was also concerned about reducing the living Christ into rigid, written laws.

Paul counseled the people of Corinth to "look not to the things that are seen but to the things that are unseen; for the things that are seen are transient, but the things that are unseen are eternal" (2 Corinthians 4.18). In the same letter he advised them to "walk by faith and not by sight" (2 Corinthians 5.7).

Paul's distinction between writing and speaking has been studied by Werner Kelber in his book *The Oral and the Written Gospel*.[2] Kelber proposed that when Paul referred to the spirit and the letter of the law he was not exclusively addressing the work-character of the law. His objection was not to the law (*nomos*) as a legal authority, but rather to the objectification of the law as writing (*gramma*). It is writing itself, *gramma*, that kills. It confines. It reduces. It enslaves the power of oral, direct communication. The term *nomos* is not even present in the third chapter of Paul's second letter to the church at Corinth.

Paul wrote to the people of Corinth that they do not need letters of recommendation from Christ or Paul. Christ's reality should be "written not with ink but with the Spirit of the living God, not on tablets of stone but on tablets of human hearts" (2 Corinthians 3.2–3).

The RSV translation of *pneuma* (spirit) and *gramma* in 2 Corinthians 3.1–6 has been informed by theological orientations that have not always paid full attention to underlying hermeneutical tensions. The RSV translation, for example, renders *to gramma* as "the written code." The term "code," arbitrarily injected by the translator, includes a range of meanings, from a set of prearranged symbols to a systematized body of law. Kelber has suggested that interpreters frequently have seized upon the law aspect, slanting Paul's hermeneutical concept of *gramma* in the direction of legalism and legalistic self-righteousness rather than indicating Paul's concern about writing itself.[3]

Paul and others during this period seem to have been wrestling with whether or not Jesus' message should remain an oral tradition or be written down. Reducing Mark's story of Jesus to writing was probably not completed until about forty years after Jesus' death. During that time the violent struggle between the Jews and Romans, A.D. 66–74, had taken place, culminating with the agony of the destruction of the Temple and Jerusalem in A.D. 70. The shame of Roman victory was compounded by the loss of the center of Jewish life and worship. Many priceless scrolls were lost forever, and nearly all the teachers were killed.

It was under this kind of pressure that in Yavneh (Jamnia) around A.D. 95–100, under the influence of Rabban Yochanan ben Zakkai and his disciples, sages met and gave the Jewish scriptures their final form. Josephus wrote that the final collection of writings was composed of twenty-four parts (thirty-nine books), divided into the Torah, the prophets, and the writings. It was not until the fourth century that the Christian canon, including the Jewish scriptures, was closed after a long process of usage by the church.

Limiting the authorized writings was the church's way of saying that this set of writings had a wholeness. The canon provided the frame or paradigm within which the faithful could find the presence of God and preserve the church's identity. This is not to say that these writings are a whole that is consistent in concept and form. The opposite is true. The corpus of sacred writings is a whole of irreducibly different parts. This is true not only of the Christian canon in its entirety but of the Gospels in particular.

Mark's writing down of the Jesus story after about three decades of oral transmission is especially interesting. It begins with the curious statement that he is writing down a "gospel." A gospel is an oral announcement. Matthew, Luke, and John did not choose to call their written stories gospels. Mark seems to be intent on keeping the oral flavor despite the written form. Perhaps Mark's story was written to be read out loud as if it still were being told.

There was no reason to write the message of Jesus exclusively in story form. The writer of the noncanonical Gospel of Thomas did not. That document, found with many others near Nag Hammadi in central Egypt around 1945, is a Coptic Gnostic collection of 114 of Jesus' sayings. No effort was made to turn them into a story.

Storytellers tell stories their own way. What we have received as the gospel is a written collection of four stories that play against one another, keeping Christ's presence as alive and storylike as it can be after having been written down in lines on papyrus centuries ago.

In the four canonical stories of Jesus there is only one time (John 8.6) when Jesus himself is pictured in the act of writing something down. The scribes and the Pharisees brought to him a woman who had been found in adultery. They challenged Jesus with an interpretation of the Law of Moses that held the woman should be stoned.

What did Jesus do? He bent down and wrote with his finger on the ground. They continued to challenge him until he

stood up and said to them, "Let him who is without sin among
you be the first to throw a stone at her" (John 8.6–7).

The people went away, one by one, and finally Jesus was
left alone with the woman. He looked up and said, "Woman,
where are they? Has no one condemned you?" She said, "No
one, Lord."

"Neither do I condemn you; go, and do not sin again."

Those who had come to catch him were themselves caught
by his parabolic act and oral challenge. The irony of writing in
the dust warned them not to enclose the Law's living presence
in written form. Jesus wrote in the dust to show that respect for
writing should not lend unwarranted authority to it and that a
statement is not absolute just because it is written down. Writing down something does not prove anything. How it is applied
is what is important. To live knowledge one needs to know its
spirit rather than the dead, written remnant of some past action. One must have the ears to hear, not the eyes to read, this
invisible and holy spirit.

This is why I have been practicing a kind of Christian education that invites children into sacred stories, parables, and
liturgical actions presented to them in a spoken way. This
method is in contrast to reading, being read to, remembering,
writing answers, watching on television, or treating scripture as
an end in itself.

Godly play, furthermore, contrasts talking *about* scripture
and worship with being *in* scripture and worship. When we
teach what is written down, we tend to talk about what the written text has said. What the written text has said is secondhand
experience. Ethics comes from the primary experience of our
deep identity. It does not come from the analytical dance of the
intelligence across pages of ink and paper. To do what is just
takes more than conceptual assent. It takes the motive power of
fundamental, spontaneous identity. The more difficult the ethical question, the more this is true.

Scripture is an invitation into the larger reality where deep
identity is formed and ethical action is rooted rather than an invitation into the world of pages, letters, lines, and book covers
that confine life. God can be discovered in books, but scripture
told out of the primary experience of love for such tales as tools

for discovery is more opening and encouraging to the creative process out of which our identity comes.

The danger of spoken communication is that it can stir the depths of irrationality and hatred as well as the love that comes from the living God. Writing is an aid to protect us against such danger. It is ironic that we must be on guard against the protection writing gives us as well as against what it protects us from. To understand this better we need to explore in additional detail the difference between written and spoken communication.

When someone physically present speaks to us, we can make judgments on many levels about our trust of the speaker. These judgments in turn help us to evaluate what is spoken. When we read, the writer is absent, so we must make up our mind about the writing in other ways. The message is exterior to the writer and must stand for itself on the page.

When the speaker is present, we can receive cues from his or her face during the telling—a twinkle in the eye, a frown on the forehead. A shrug of the shoulders or clenched fists and a set jaw "speak" louder than the words that are said. These physical signs are lost in the written text, which provides its own kind of context, whatever the writer originally may have had in mind.

One of the most important differences between oral and written communication has to do with silence. Silence has different functions in speaking and writing. When one is listening to someone who is present, a span of silence is not empty of meaning. In oral communication the speaker remains present and in control of the silence. When the message is written, there is nothing to sustain the communication during silence.

When you stop reading, the communication stops. You might go on thinking about what you have already read, but the primary act of decoding the message stops. In the world of writing the control of the silence is in the reader. It is not controlled by the one who originates the communication, as it is in the world of speaking.

Speaking and listening need special memory markers, such as Homer's "wine-dark sea," and shapers, such as "Let me make one thing perfectly clear," to make the communication memorable and to give it auditory form. Speakers need to repeat more, to use multiple ways of saying the same thing, and to review the structure of the message to indicate to the listener where the message is going and where it has come from at any given moment. This is true whether the communication is a story, a lecture, a poem, or some other form. In contrast, if the message is in writing, one can review and find one's place at will.

Speaking is more situational than writing. The storyteller shapes the story to the audience. A public speaker uses different illustrations for the same themes when confronted by different groups of listeners. The written message, however, remains the same, fixed on the page, regardless of the audience. The writer can write for a predicted audience, but if that audience is not present the writing cannot adjust itself.

Listening is by nature a public experience. The speaker and the listener must both be present. Reading can be solitary. The written text can help you imagine others, including the author, to keep you company, but spoken communication is done with others actually present. This gives opportunity for side comments among the audience and permits the response of the audience to help shape the message itself.

Oral communication requires effort by the listener to remember what is being said while listening. Written communication allows the reader to ponder interpretations during the reading of the message, since the text is fixed. Accuracy, footnotes, and other apparatus are provided to give the text its own kind of authority and to resist the reinterpretations that are possible because of the text's stability. Speaking's authority comes more from the speaker's interaction with the audience.

The face-to-face quality of oral communication is very different from the faceless written word. Writing communicates more quickly, more clearly, and more permanently. When the speaker stops speaking, what has been said is gone, except for what is remembered, often in different ways by different listeners.

Important for our purposes, the quality of the imagination is different in written and oral communication. To enter into a story or oral message, one needs to give up control. One actively orients within the spoken story's time and space during the conveying of the communication. This stirs the imagination in a more right-brained way. The linear thinking that assimilates lines on paper is more left-brained.

The oral style of communication is best for opening up the creative process and playing with ideas. Writing is the better way to evaluate new ideas and form judgments about them. Listening leaves one more vulnerable to change. Writing fixes the text and is better for holding fast to what has been said in the past. We need both to keep our religious identity and to remain alive.

THE SPOKEN LESSON AND TELEVISION

Many parents today are struggling to know what to teach their children about the ultimate realities of life. These adults carry with them, however, a lot pain and conflict or boredom and frustration from their own religious upbringing. This makes them pause for a time about what to do. During this time of indecision the television stands ready, and most likely turned on, to fill the void. Into the unintentional vacuum pours a flood of electronic signals teaching children who they are and what is ultimately real. This televised religious education by default is why Godly play is so important at this moment in human history.

In 1981 Gregor Goethals wrote:

> To live today in the awareness of a mystical,
> transcendent order of being and of unknown
> dimensions of time and human experience opens up
> fearful and undreamed-of worlds. These realities
> are frightening, for they awaken us from a sleep we
> had not known as sleep. It is much easier to pull the
> covers of culture over our heads and sleep a little
> longer before awakening. It is much easier to watch
> the world turn on soaps and stay tuned to the Super
> Bowl.[5]

The television set sits at the center of our culture's living room as the common denominator of communication. It provides a ritual for gathering and orders time by its programming. It entertains us by its stories. It is, however, seldom

parabolic. The medium, as it is used commercially, is not inclined to point out its own limitations. Instead, it hypnotizes us
and suggests its own version of reality.

The ascension of television as a teacher of reality is a new
chapter in an old story. Television now holds the importance
once held by printed books, and before that, by handwritten
manuscripts and storytellers. Today the "letter" that confines
and kills the spirit is not written on papyrus strips or printed in
thick books. It comes to us in buzzing images on television and
computer screens, such as the one I am looking at now as I
write this sentence.

Events have been rushing by us with extreme speed. In
1920 Vladimir Zworykin patented the iconoscope, an all-elec-
tric television tube. Seven years later AT&T sent a closed cir-
cuit television picture from Washington to New York.

In 1939 NBC began offering regular telecasting schedules.
In the forty years from 1939 to 1979 television literally
changed the world by changing how we view the world. Instead
of looking out the window or going out the door, people began
to turn on the television set. Just counting the increasing number of television sets in homes suggests the vastness of this media shift.

By 1948 there were nearly 500,000 television sets in the
United States. In 1956 television momentarily surpassed news-
papers, magazines, and radio in total advertising revenue. By
1960 there were 533 stations and 55 million television sets.
Ten years later there were 690 stations and 85 million sets. By
1978 there were 974 stations and too many sets to count. The
revenues from advertising had reached $6 billion.

At the close of the first forty years of rapid growth
(1939–1979) 98 percent of all households in the United States
had television sets—more households than had adequate diets
or indoor plumbing. Color television was in 83 percent of all
households and 49 percent of our homes had more than one
television set.

The speed and excitement of this change has obscured
how vast a media shift this has been and how it has changed our
view of reality. We need to step back and look at other such
changes to get a better view of what is going on as television

teaches religion as much by *how it teaches* as by what it teaches. To tell the story of media and religion we will focus on the Bible, and follow the outline of Thomas E. Boomershine's research.[6]

✴ In the Judeo-Christian tradition God spoke first. The world was brought into being by God's word and the creation of nature was the first story. God also wrote first and writing transformed the laws of life into a permanent text. The first indication of writing in the Bible was when God wrote on the stone tablets given to Moses (Exodus 25.12). The tablets were so sacred they were placed in the Ark, which was set apart from ordinary space first in the tent in the desert and then in the Jerusalem temple, built by King Solomon. Even within the sacred space of the tent and temple the container of the written law, the Ark, was further set apart in the Holy of Holies.

The first recorded public reading of a manuscript was Josiah's reading of the Deuteronomy scroll in 622 B.C. (1 Kings 22). In 605 B.C. the first explicit act of media resistance took place: Jehoiakim fed Jeremiah's scroll into a brazier to be burned piece by piece. Each media shift is accompanied by some form of resistance to it.

About 444 B.C. Ezra became the first master of the new medium to lead Israel. He read the Torah one morning at the Water Gate. This was the central action of covenant renewal. According to Nehemiah (9.8), the Levites interpreted the Law as he read. A new pattern of community organization was established. The reading aloud of sacred texts, accompanied by oral interpretation, is the deep root of worship in the synagogue and the Christian church.

Writing became the dominant culture of Athens and was spread across the East by the conquests of Alexander the Great. He died in 323 B.C. without ever returning to Greece, but the impact of writing lasted long after his conquests were divided up and disappeared.

In the first century A.D. the changes writing had brought to Israel helped break apart the Jews and the Jewish-Christians. After the destruction of the Temple in A.D. 70 Judaism organized itself as a militantly oral tradition in which the oral law was maintained as the dominant form of thinking. Christian

Judaism (Christianity) reformed its communities of worship around the new way of thinking related to writing and reading.

In the age of the manuscript, the Bible became a book. Public readings of holy manuscripts gave power to those who could interpret the signs on paper into the spoken sounds of public speech. Scripture was sung, chanted, and read in a stylized way. The process of interpretation involved identifying the ideas that were implicit in the readings. These ideas were then discussed in the categories of theology in a way similar to the practice of Greco-Roman rhetoric. God was now experienced less as a character in story and more as a Being or Essence. God became omniscient, omnipotent, and omnipresent.

With the rise of medieval universities a difference appeared between the reading that took place among monks in the rural monasteries and the reading that took place among scholars in the universities in the cities. According to Jean Leclercq, O.S.B., this difference began to appear during the twelfth century.[7]

The monks outside the city read actively, pronouncing the words in a low tone. Scripture was not studied for its own sake as it was in the university; it was studied for the benefit of the reader and usually in the context of the liturgy. Rather than challenging the text with questions as the scholars did, the monks ruminated and used their imaginations to make scripture come to life. The Bible was not commented on by way of concepts or themes but by what Leclercq called an "exegesis by concordance."

The way the rural monks interpreted the Bible was closer to that of the rabbis than to that of the Christian university scholars. The scriptures had become so much a part of their memories and imaginations that any passage fired associations that branched out into all parts of scripture. The images deepened one another rather than becoming the objects of analysis.

In the fifteenth century a new medium for scripture appeared. Gutenberg invented the movable press in the 1440s and printed his first Bible no later than 1455. The birth of the print culture put great pressure on the church and contributed to the Reformation. The Roman Church bitterly opposed the printing and distribution of the scriptures, particularly in vernacular translations. Protestants appropriated the new medium at once and used it as an aid to resist the authority of the pope and to help reform the church. Gradually, especially because of the leadership of the Jesuits, the Roman Catholic community also appropriated the new medium. Today Roman Catholics print more books than any other part of the church.

Scripture was read in a more prosaic manner in the world of print. The Bible became much more available. Now it could be heard read aloud in family circles and other small groups. After the Reformation, patterns of community formed around the Bible that fractured the wholeness of the church even more. Both public and private readings moved away from the allegorical interpretation of the medieval period. The pattern of interpretation became more literal. In addition, God became a matter of personal experience as people read alone or in small groups.

Silent reading developed in the seventeenth and eighteenth centuries in Europe and in the eighteenth and nineteenth centuries in the United States. The sign of this change can be identified by the way the author addressed the reader. Medieval literature addressed the reader as a listener ("Listen, lordings") until the sixteenth century. In the fiction of Fielding and Sterne, the form of address became "Dear reader." Writing had become associated primarily with the eyes rather than with the ears.

The system of interpretation that developed in the visual print culture turned the Bible into a document with black (and sometimes red) marks on the page. The study of the Bible became textual criticism. Biblical history and biblical theology emerged. The "eternal now" of scripture was fractured and held at a distance. Written history was elevated as the locus of authority.

The study of ancient biblical documents takes place in silence, usually in the library. Scholars produce books and articles that are also to be read in silence. A major exception to this process is in public worship. The reading of scripture and its oral interpretation in a sermon are all that is left today of the public reading and commentary begun by Ezra almost 2,500 years ago. It is ironic that only sermons of special merit are printed today.

Increasingly, however, it is television and not print, writing, or storytelling that shapes and lends authority to religion. In 1949 the first national religious television program, ABC's prime-time series "I Believe," appeared. Many religious leaders rushed to use television just as the Protestants had rushed to use the new medium of print in the sixteenth century.

The enthusiasm for religious television in our time has resulted in an electronic Bible. Rather than pages of print, this new Bible has taken the form of evangelical talk shows and high-powered sermons preached to large congregations.

When the Bible is presented on the screen as if one were in worship, the camera moves back and forth across the congregation, giving the viewer a sense of the occasion's drama and shared importance. The video version of worship and the Bible, however, is vastly different from the real version. The receiver of these sounds and images is often a solitary, silent individual rather than a living congregation.

There is a second difference between video worship and its Bible and the living congregation's encounter with scripture. The video framing of worship and scripture narrows the Bible to what can be effective in terms of positive financial and viewing response. As with secular television, what is not successful in terms of ratings and money disappears from the tube.

What people need to hear from scripture is often not what they want to hear, so the Bible cannot help but be truncated by television. One task of Godly play is to balance sacred story, liturgy, and parable so that the whole domain of Christian language can be preserved to do its work.

In 1973 Harvey Cox's book *The Seduction of the Spirit*[8] signaled the danger of religion propagated by the mass media. He said that the signals pose as stories. They pretend to be something other than they are. They use our spiritual needs for the ends of the one who is purchasing the signals. The language of seducers is hidden in the gesture of dialogue, trust, intimacy, and personal rapport. The danger is that the communication is not to nourish the human community but is to undermine it.

Television's sounds and images seem to fill our sacramental needs and our need for a story. An additional danger is that television's impression of liturgy and its stories will distract us from the master story. We need the master story to help us find meaning for our personal stories. Television also diverts us from the uneasy questions raised by the parabolic.

Television can expand our world, but it can also contract it. Our global habitat has been seen from the moon, but regional variety has been blurred into one bland manner of speaking and a uniform picture of how to clothe, bathe, and deodorize ourselves. Both the enlarged and the narrowed version of the world television gives us remains electronic rather than living, and this is the problem for religious education. The television self, the television others, the television earth, and the television god cannot respond to us. Godly play can put us in touch with ourselves, others, nature, and God, because it can respond to the individual uniqueness of persons and situations. Television has little such flexibility, despite its many virtues.

Television teaches us to be viewers who receive passively the excitement of vicarious human adventure rather than the reality of personal, living heroism. It saps the energy it takes to venture into the wilderness to find our own way toward God in the company of living pilgrims. It even diverts us from the direct experience of our own families and draws us into the lives of electronic families. Godly play reverses this trend and invites us into the wilderness to make our own pilgrimage and asks us to not only make contact with God but also with our true selves, our families (and family of families, the church), and with nature.

Godly play is needed today to provide an alternative to television as the primary teacher of children and adults about religion. Most of television's teaching goes on by default rather than by design, but the result is the same. A direct, active encounter with the Creator in the midst of real nature, real people, and the real self is obscured by television's electronic reality.

Most important, the one-way communication of television forces us to conform to it. It cannot support the creative process of each unique viewer. The tube cannot play. It is not free in the way human beings are. It is too predictable (fifteen-minute segments and worn-out plots). There is too much control (switching channels), and at the same time too little control (the one-way communication).

The medium of television can only teach its own medium as reality. This adds yet another layer of media to the written and printed communication already between us and the primary coordination of actions in life and death. Television is the right tool for many tasks, but for religious education and spiritual growth it is not. In some homes, it is all children have, but that does not mean that it is what works best for their spiritual direction.

The illusion created by the glowing tube can separate us from reality by inflating our fantasy rather than feeding our imagination with reality. This is the unspoken lesson of the electronic images for religion. The televised images are not directly embedded in the reality of the self, other people, the earth, and God, so how can television teach us the unspoken lesson of how to know reality better?

My warning about televised religious education by default is not an unthinking act of media resistance. It is a caution that the electronic Bible is unable, by itself, to support our growth and development as creators of religious meaning. [Television cannot teach the art of using religious language because the unspoken lesson of television is that we must passively receive its one-way communication] It invites us to absorb rather than to create. By contrast, the unspoken lesson of Godly play is that we are born to be creators in the image of our Maker.

Television dramatically raises the problem of the unspoken lesson. *How* we communicate is at least as important as *what* we communicate about religion. We turn now to an examination of the unspoken lesson in Godly play and how it supports the creative process. The next chapter is devoted to this discussion.

5 The Unspoken Lesson

Godly play attempts to create a situation where wonder, community, an awareness of existential limits, religious language, the creative process, and the structure of the Holy Eucharist work together to enable the child to enter religious language in order to make meaning and find direction with God in life and death. The triangle of wonder, the creative process, and the existential limits have already been presented as the key features of the spoken lesson. We turn now to the Holy Eucharist structure, the community structure of relationships and ethics, and the structuring of the classroom's space by the functions of religious language.

Holy Eucharist — Community/Ethics

Religious Language

We will proceed by asking three questions. How does the organization of space in the classroom teach? How does the time spent in the classroom teach? How do the people in the classroom teach when they are not speaking?

TEACHING WITH SPACE

When we walk into a room, the colors, the arrangement of the furniture, the light, the odors, the noise, the taste on the tip of the tongue, the shape of the room, and other perceptions combine to "speak" to us. We notice how the room is cared for. Is it clean and orderly? Are things torn or broken? We notice much more than we can make an inventory of, but what this all adds up to is the sum of the values that are embedded in the room. This is why the church has always been careful about the arrangement of space within the worship area. We need to be even more careful with the environment in which we teach the art of using the language by which we worship.

The environment is at work communicating even when we are not attending to its communication. Children are even more vulnerable to this communication than we adults are. At some level they notice whether the room is clean, orderly, and in good repair. This communicates to them whether the people in charge of the room really care about the place they have entered. That in turn suggests to the children whether they will be cared for there or not.

Children cannot focus very well on the learning task when the room about them is always changing. They need a steady, stable environment to deal best with the changes of learning. They need an orderly background against which to discover something new. Young children cannot hold words, ideas, or the environment as firmly in their minds as adults can, so stability is especially important for the little ones.

One of the ways to discover how your classroom looks to a child is to take a child's-eye view of it. Get down at a child's eye level and get comfortable. Begin to look around. Let the room soak in.

This is not an exercise to tell whether you are a good teacher or not. It is not a way to *think* about the room. It is a time for feelings. Let them come. Does the room feel warm and welcoming? Can you feel yourself relax and open up by the way the room takes you in? Does the arrangement of space actually emphasize what you value most in the room?

Go sit in the doorway. What do the children see first when

they enter the room? Is that focal object the central, organizing point of value for the room's purpose? This is why in many churches you see the altar first when you enter through the front door. This is why in my classroom the "altar-shelf" is what the child sees first.

I already described the altar shelf in chapter 1, but I would like to remind you of that here, and expand on the previous description a bit. The Holy Family sits in the middle of the top shelf on the color of the liturgical season. Behind the Holy Family is the risen Christ. To the right is the Good Shepherd, and to the left is the Light. These are images Jesus gave to people when they asked him who he was. "I am the Good Shepherd," he said. Another time he said, "I am the Light."

The primary images on the top shelf lead the eye to the shelves below. In the center shelf, under the Holy Family, are the colored cloths of the other liturgical seasons and the materials about the circle of the church year. In the center of the bottom shelf are lessons about the saints, because saints' days are organized into the liturgical year to keep their lives alive to guide and inspire us.

Beneath the Good Shepherd who stands to the right of the Holy Family is a lesson about Holy Communion. The green circle of the Good Shepherd on the top shelf is put next to the green circle on the second shelf when the Good Shepherd lesson is presented to the children. The Shepherd leads the sheep out of the sheepfold on the first circle to the table that is in the center of the second circle. On the third shelf, below the two circles of green, is the basket of people, representing the people of the world, who replace the sheep around the table.

Beneath the Light that stands to the left of the Holy Family are the lessons on Baptism. The sensorial materials—a bowl, a pitcher for filling the bowl with water, a candle snuffer, and a doll—are on a tray on the second shelf. The candle from the top shelf is used for the paschal candle. On the third shelf are the prayer book and a set of cards with labels that identify the significant symbols and gestures for the Liturgy of Baptism. There are also extra candles for the Liturgy of the Light, which invites the children in the circle to remember when they received their light on the day of their baptism.

The focal point of the room shows Christ as the center. Christ's presence is deepened, to either side, by the images of the responses he made about his own identity. His responses lead us to the two major sacraments, Baptism and Holy Communion. This anchors the room's meaning.

Another anchor for the room's meaning is the team of adults. We will discuss them more in a few moments, but *where* those people are in the room has a great deal to do with the meaning they communicate. This is in addition to *how* they do what they do.

The storyteller sits in front of the altar shelf. This person embodies the story, parable, and liturgical action. The meaning that is incarnate in the person who sits by the door is as important but different. It has to do with welcoming and saying good-bye. It helps to draw the line at the door between ordinary language and experience and the language and experience being shown and used in the classroom.

The storyteller organizes the circle and brings focus to the embodiment of the art. The door person welcomes the children, helps them get ready, helps with the art responses, helps prepare the classroom for the feast, and helps with the good-byes. Neither person can do his or her job without the other.

When it is time for the children to get out their own work, they are dismissed from the circle one at a time. This gives the door person a chance to help each child stay focused on the task chosen, so the children can continue to move with intention from the circle to the room's larger environment. While the door person is supporting the children in their choices, the storyteller maintains the circle and helps the remaining children be patient while waiting their turns. The presenter also helps them take an interest in one another's work.

The circle itself is a space of great importance. The circle of children indirectly includes the teachers, but these adults must also take a leadership role. The door person remains by the door unless there is an emergency in the circle. The role of the presenter is not to take possession of the lesson but to go to the shelf and bring the lesson to the circle for that community—

the children and the adult presenter—to make meaning with. This is an open-access curriculum. It shows how to use a set of tools (language) to build something (a world).

The presenter puts the lesson in the middle of the circle. The presenter shows how to "enter" the lesson rather than telling the children how to think about it or what answer it should be reduced to. This shows respect for each member of the circle and an awareness of each one's own journey.

The circle is where the invisible words of religion become visible. It is like a small church. This is why such care is taken to enter and leave the circle with respect and why relationships are given such attention. There is never a day, regardless of the lesson, that ethics is not taught. It is taught by how the teacher models and supports relationships with the children. How we are with one another is our ethics, so we need to be careful to teach and be the ethics we mean to teach. Children need limits, for example, and appropriate words to begin to include the perspective of other children in their thoughts and actions.

Caring for one another is related to caring for the environment. God gave us the great gift of the creation to care about and take care of. We walk on holy ground. If we do not care for one another and what is at hand in the environment directly about us, the classroom, how can we expect children to care for and take care of the whole of creation, "our island home," when they grow up?

Showing how to get out one's work and how to put it away is a lesson about the value of our identity as God's creatures in this wonder of creation. It is not just picking up and putting away. Taking care to clean up or to walk around another child's work spread out on the floor is a form of caring for one another and the environment. It is a way of valuing respect for others, their work, and God's world.

People sometimes feel inadequate or frustrated by the criticism that Sunday school only *talks* about life and does nothing about it. This is clearly a misunderstanding. The criticism is blind to the way space in the environment teaches. When we ask children to get dressed up and come to a special place on a special day, we must be careful, for we are teaching something.

The question always is, What is the hidden curriculum? Does it match what we intend to teach? Do the spoken and the unspoken lesson teach the same values?

The shelves in the room are arranged to distinguish the subfunctions of the religious language system. Each shelf unit is constructed the same way to show that, although the subfunctions are different, they are of equal value. The level of the shelves in each system is also an intentional use of space.

The top shelf holds the most sensorial and most important images for the child. For example, the guiding parables are placed there in their gold boxes. The materials set on the lower shelves are not the parables of Jesus. None of these are in gold boxes.

There is also a movement toward abstraction as one moves from the top shelves down to the lower shelves in the sacred story and parable shelf systems. For example, the set of gold cards that includes most of Jesus' parables is located on the lower shelves of the parable shelf unit. On the same shelf are guiding cards that show how to play different kinds of games concerning the whole collection of parables. There are even materials about the sayings of Jesus there. They are connected with the wisdom sayings and laws that summarize the sacred stories.

The sacred story shelves work the same way, but the materials on the top shelf are quite different from the gold parable boxes sitting on top of the parable shelves. The sacred story lessons sit on their own trays, which help organize them in a sensorimotor way. The trays, of course, also give the child the means to carry the whole set of materials to the rug, the desert box, or wherever the lesson will be worked with.

The Old Testament shelves begin with the lesson about the Creation, and the New Testament shelves end with a lesson about the part of the story that hasn't been told yet. They run along one wall from alpha to omega, beginning to end. A different kind of shelf unit stands between the Old Testament and the New Testament shelves. It holds the desert box and the lessons about Hebrew and Greek. Its position between the Old and New Testament shelves shows the change of languages and worlds.

An example of a sacred story material is the lesson for the Exodus. The tray includes a basket to hold the People of God. There are also two blue pieces of felt rolled up. The principle employed is that "less is more." Like the parables and other materials, the sacred story can tell itself to all ages and stages if the material makes the core of the event present.

To see what the child does, imagine a young girl. She goes to get out a rug from the rug box, takes it over to where the desert box is, and places it underneath the box. As I described earlier, the desert box is a clear, shallow plastic box with a lid that contains sand. ("So many important things happen in the desert that we just have to have a piece of the desert in the classroom," I say to the children.) When the box is pulled out from its special shelf section and is resting on the rug, the children can pull the rug to the place where they want to work. This helps them get out their own work, despite the problem of the heavy sand tray. The struggle with the weight of the sand makes this really "big work."

Next, our little girl goes to the sacred story shelves and gets the tray for the Exodus. She puts the people in the desert and moves them through the story as the presenter has shown in a lesson in the circle or as she has seen another child do who has already had the lesson. The rule is that the children can work with any material in the classroom, provided they have had the lesson first.

This rule makes it clear that the materials are not for free play. The freedom comes in the response to the sacred story, parable, or liturgical material. If the children were allowed to change the material's use, then there would be nothing left for them to use from religious language to make meaning with.

Let us return to the Exodus lesson. The blue pieces of felt are rolled out, and the people are "pressed against the water" by Pharaoh's army. The two pieces are rolled back slightly to allow the People of God "to pass through the water into freedom."

When the people are all on the other side, they are free! Miriam leads the dancing. The blue felt is rolled closed, and the people are put into a circle with Miriam in the center. The discussion about the destruction of Pharaoh's army is left for later. If someone raises the point, the presenter tells the Jewish legend of the laughing angels being silenced by God. God told the angels that when any creature of God's creation is injured or dies, God weeps.

The girl working with the lesson of the Exodus in the desert box puts away her work before the lesson is considered finished. The parts of the lesson go back on the tray with care and respect. The tray is carried with two hands to its place on the top shelf of the sacred story shelves. The desert box is dragged back to its place and the plastic box is slid back onto the lower shelf of that part of the shelf system.

The lower levels of the sacred story shelves are filled with follow-up materials. Books, photographs, maps, and other things are there to clarify the relevant geography, history, and culture, expanding the lessons for the older children. Here, too, are materials for following the story of the church to the present day. This is a place where a child can even find a lesson by which to tell his or her own story.

The liturgical shelves extend beyond the altar shelf. On one side of the focal or altar shelf is a set of shelves that contain the Christmas materials. On the other side of the focal shelf is a set of shelves that contain the lessons on Easter. A shelf section for Pentecost remains to be created and tested. Each of these three major Sundays of the liturgical year should be represented in the space of the classroom. Work on this is now under way at the Children's Center. There is also an overflow shelf that contains more materials about the saints, since they can't all fit into the altar shelf's lower center section that holds the materials about the circle of the church year.

Near the liturgical shelves is a whole setup for preparing the altar for Holy Communion. It includes a sacristy cupboard, a small altar, a pulpit, a lectern, a tabernacle fastened to the wall, and a credence shelf fastened to the wall to its right. There is a set of labels that goes with this for the older children. The labeling helps confirm the naming of the many hangings, cloths, and vessels.

There is also a section of shelves that holds the art materials, such as paints, clay, and other supplies. Shelves filled with books for the older children have Bibles and resource books.

This is also where the lessons on the history of the writing of the Bible are kept.

We turn now to the discussion of how time teaches in the classroom, expanding on what has been said or implied in previous chapters.

TEACHING WITH TIME

The famous "forty-five–minute hour" has already been mentioned. Some think it is too long a time, and some think it is too short. There are those who don't care about the time as long as the Sunday school provides baby-sitting so they can go to adult education or church. Others view Sunday school as "what's done," so they do it. A few have a vague sense that it is important but can't say why. Still others see it as a golden opportunity.

The rhythm of church school time is related to what has been discovered over the centuries as a structure that opens up communication with God in an optimum way for a religious community. This is true for a community of children as well as adults. It also bears some general likeness to the pattern by which the creative process flows. (The pattern of the imagination in action will be discussed in chapter 6.)

The structure of time for a class has these four steps:

1. *Coming in*
   a. Entering the special space
   b. Getting ready

4. *Going out*
   a. Saying good-bye
   b. Leaving the special place

2. *Hearing the Word of God*
   a. Participation in the lesson
   b. Responding to the lesson

3. *Sharing Holy Communion*
   a. Preparing the feast
   b. Sharing the feast

Urban T. Holmes used the work of Victor Turner to describe the need for pilgrimage outside normal social structures in order to encounter God in the wilderness and chaos of the "antistructure."[1] The structures of society work to insulate one from the mystery of God and dilute the power of such an encounter. To step across the threshold of the classroom is to enter a "place of imagining," in Holmes's words. A different language is spoken here. Relationships are attended to in a careful and caring way to promote both the learning and use of that language to know God.

Holmes spoke of the time of pilgrimage as a form of play. The true pilgrim is childlike. It is a dangerous time, for it is a time of ambiguity and imagination. Pilgrims require a strong structure of symbols and rituals to keep from being overwhelmed on their journey.

The children's journey into the classroom is a pilgrimage into a wilderness of antistructure when compared to the structure of their normal life at home and school or child care. This wilderness is not chaos, however. It is structured in such a way that the child or the adult will not be overcome. It is a safe place in which to engage the imagination about the darker and wilder side of life in order to create a constructive world of action to overcome such destructive forces.

The reason this can be accomplished in the classroom is that the classroom time includes a time of dependence and a time of independence. Even the time of independence, the time of wondering and response, is carefully structured so that any child who wishes to can opt out. This kind of "oscillation" in the structuring of the time is important for growth, as Bruce Reed discussed in his book *The Dynamics of Religion.*[2]

The oscillation Reed described is between periods of autonomous activity and periods of physical or symbolic contact with sources of renewal. It is a shifting back and forth between being dependent on a trusted other and actively exploring the world. We all venture out like children ranging out into the park in play, but from time to time we need to come running back to Mother for renewal. We can then go running off again merrily on our own. Sometimes we need to regress to go forward.

Hard decisions need to be made every Sunday morning about the care of time so that it can teach what we mean for it to teach. Sometimes it is so hard for the children to become peaceful and collected that a great deal of time is needed to build the circle. The price is that expanding circle time squeezes out time for the formal, spoken lesson.

On a day when it takes about fifteen minutes to build a circle where everyone can get ready, the teacher might choose to skip the lesson and go on to an unrushed, careful preparation and sharing of the feast, followed by the good-byes. In such a situation the theme of Holy Communion, blessing, and dismissal would be emphasized over the theme of the Liturgy of the Word.

Another Sunday there might be time for a lesson but not for a response to it. The lack of time for a response to lessons might build up over several Sundays. Finally, the teacher can set aside a Sunday when the class goes right to a response without any lesson. We call these "work days." This may be a poor choice of words, since it implies that on other days we do not do important work, but "response days" and other alternatives sounded too artificial and clinical.

At other times the lesson and the responses are going so well that there is no time for the feast. At still other times one might squeeze in the feast and squeeze out time for a careful saying of good-bye. All kinds of combinations can arise, and each decision is hard to make.

The importance of saying good-bye should not be overlooked. The door person calls each child's name when the parent is present outside the door. Only names of children who are ready are called. The child whose name has been called comes up close to the presenter. The presenter takes the child by the hands and talks privately about the good work the child has done that day and how the child is such a good person. This gives the presenter an opportunity to have a brief but private conversation with each child that might otherwise be neglected. This is especially important on days when the presenter has had to be very clear with a few of the children to keep the limits of behavior clearly drawn so they include only constructive action.

We turn now to a discussion of the people involved in the teaching. This discussion is not about what they teach but about how they teach. The nonverbal "lesson" focused on here is the one given by the teaching team every Sunday, whether they think about it consciously or not.

TEACHING WITH PEOPLE

This is not about what people say in the classroom. It is about
what they do and how they feel. It is about how they see the
children and how they fit into what they see. The unit of observation for this kind of teaching is the group of children and
adults as a whole. An intervention at any point in this network
of relationships affects the whole group, including the person
who made the change.

Supporting the Whole Group

Adults can control groups of children. That is not hard. It can
be done by force, by threats, by guilt, by shame, by making
deals, and by other means. Clearly, the most appropriate way to
communicate with God is not taught in such a manner. Only a
religion of control, threat, fear, force, authority, suspicion,
guilt, and shame is taught this way. To know God we need to
help one another. We need to work through the whole group
to help each member of the community of faith move toward
the Creator.

It is sometimes difficult for adults to work through the community of children to help individual children be more constructive in their spiritual development and use of religious language.
There is a sense of power one can get from controlling individuals or groups that is not available to the adults by this means.
To enable the group to be more creative and alive, one must become the servant of the group and almost disappear in it. Praise
is no longer directed to the teacher. It is directed to the children
who are working on their own within carefully crafted, clear,
constructive limits. This means that the art they learn, the experience of the community, and the experience of God, is theirs. It
is primary. It is not a secondary kind of hearsay evidence filtered
through the adult's experience and told to them.

You may think that this sort of involvement in the whole
group is too vague. You may dismiss this kind of talk because it
does not seem to touch the reality of the classroom. To make
this way of being in the group clearer, let me be more specific

about the actual jobs that the members of the teaching team do during class time on a typical Sunday morning. Let us assume the class begins at about ten o'clock and ends about eleven o'clock. The activities of the door person and the presenter during this time are shown in the accompanying table.

Jobs of the Sunday-Morning Teaching Team

Door Person	*Presenter*
1. Check the material on shelves, especially the supply shelves.	1. Check material to be presented that day.
2. Get out the roll book and pencil and be ready to greet the children.	2. Get seated on the floor and get ready to greet the children.
3. Stop the children coming into the room and "talk them down" until they are ready; take roll as they come in or have the older children check themselves in.	3. Guide the children to places in the circle where it will be easiest for them to focus on the lesson. Visit quietly until all are ready.
4. Remain in the chair by the door unless a special need arises so as to help the children come to be with you until they are ready to return to the circle.	4. Present the lesson. Model how to "enter" into the metaphor and flow of sacred story, parable, or liturgical material.
5. Do not make eye contact with the presenter so as to avoid breaking his or her concentration or creating a sense of the two adults talking down to or manipulating the children.	5. Once the lesson is moving, model how to "enter" into the flow and metaphor of the lesson. Avoid eye contact with the children unless necessary so they can focus on the lesson and not on the presenter.
6. When the children choose work and leave the circle, be ready to help them set up their art materials.	6. Go around the circle asking what work each child would like to get out. Dismiss each one when he or she knows and can move with intention. Keep going around the circle

7. Help the children who need
help, balancing that with
remaining in your chair so as
not to intrude in the
community of children as
they work.

8. When children are called to
the line, notice the first ones
who are ready or keep a list
to decide how to select
helpers for the feast.

9. Help the children serve the
feast. Have the drinks served
last by the most mature
children, or serve them
yourself.

10. Sit quietly in your chair.

11. Check to be sure the trash
can has a plastic liner and
will be able to hold all the
trash from the feast.

until all who can choose have
done so. The rest need more
guidance, so they remain in
the circle for another lesson.

7. Guide the children in their
work, but avoid over-
directing. When children are
working well, go sit at your
customary place in the circle
and enjoy watching them.

8. At about 10:45 or earlier
turn off the lights and ask to
see their eyes so you can talk
to them all at once. Tell
them to put away their work.
There is plenty of time, but
they need to do it now.
When they are finished, they
should come to the circle
and get ready for the feast.

9. Sit in the circle with the
children and model being
ready and saying "Thank
you." Help the children get
ready by reminding them
that we wait until all are
served "because it is more
fun to have a feast all
together."

10. Ask for but don't pressure
prayers.

11. Show the children how to
fold their crumbs in their
napkins and put their
napkins inside the cups. If
there is liquid still in the
cups, tell the chidren that
there is a plastic liner in the
trash can, so they don't have
to worry about the juice
running out on the floor.

12. Check the area outside the door for the parents and get ready to call the names of the children whose parents are there.	12. Help the children get ready to have their names called.
13. If a child starts for the door, remind him or her to go back and tell the presenter good-bye.	13. Take the hands of each child unless it is very awkward and tell each of them in a private way that you like them; that they did good work; that they are a good boy or girl; and to come back when they can.
14. Remember to give back the things "checked at the door" when the children came in; say a small good-bye to each, and greet the parents.	14. Take time and enjoy saying good-bye to each child.
15. When all are gone, check the supply shelves.	15. When all are gone, check the material shelves.

The table gives you an idea of some of the specific tasks that make the whole system of relationships work in a creative and open way. This is a linear presentation of a nonlinear activity. It is, therefore, a misrepresentation, but it is at least a hint about what goes on when teaching with people is being done well.

The paradox of Godly play is that the ultimate goal that shapes these objectives cannot be worked toward directly. It is not something that can be accomplished by the teacher. The ultimate goal of this approach to religious education is for the children to become aware of their deep identity as creators, involved with God in the fundamental force that guides the universe.

Supporting the Creative Process

The imagination in action is the creative process. The action of the creative process has a pattern that can be identified. A teacher who has a sense of the pattern of the creative process can give each step in the process an appropriate kind of support.

The creative process is set in motion by an opening in our individual circle of meaning. The opening may be hard or soft. A hard opening is a break that comes from tragedy or other crisis. We are forced to see that the meaning by which we have lived, on whatever level, has been broken. The threat of death, the death of another, the loss of a job, or the loss of a dream are all examples of events that can cause a break in our circle of meaning. Such breaks are necessary and are not necessarily only bad. Sometimes we bring them on ourselves. Sometimes they contribute to our growth. Nevertheless, they are hard on us, and they are hard to work through.

A soft opening is clearly a break in our circle of meaning, but the way it happens is very different. A soft break comes from wonder. The frame dissolves around what we take for granted or consciously commit to as meaningful. The frame is not broken. The new picture we have grown to know, slowly or suddenly, overflows the old frame. The old frame is clearly too small, but the dimensions of the new picture are not yet certain.

Whether the break is hard or soft, the next step is a scanning of the horizon of experience to find what the new dimension of meaning might be. Sometimes this means straining language to its fullest. At other times an image from the middle range of our experience, the nearby sense of our own body or the everyday world about us, gives us an image for the new meaning.

The logic of juxtaposition, used naturally by the preschool child, is the logic of play. It is also the logic of scanning. Piaget noticed that preschool children do not have internalized structures of classification by which to sort things out in the way most adults and older children do. Preschool children juxtapose bits and pieces of the world and language in novel ways. They associate things by similar sounds or relate events that happen together by chance as being connected by cause and effect.

Adults have internalized the ordinary meanings of language and the classifications by which the world is known. While preschool children have no choice but to play with language to know it, adults need to relax the ordinary meanings they use by habit in order to play in this way during the scanning period of the creative process. A child is good at opening meaning; an adult is good at closing meaning. Everyone needs to have both tendencies to make meaning well.

The opening tendency continues until there is a shift felt with intuitive force. This shift is the turning point from the old to the new, from the inadequate frame for meaning to a reformed, renewed way of looking at the world. This might come all at once, but usually there is only the sense that something has shifted. A symbol might take on new potency. We might remember a bit of a dream with special force or become preoccupied with a daydream. The significance is not known until we expand the image into language, but we feel the shift of energy.

Scanning is not a period of relaxation. It is a period of increasing tension. Some people can tolerate this tension in the service of the new idea better than others. It is a time of chaos, and it is uncomfortable; to some, it is intolerable. Some people try to live with the old meaning that has been broken and pretend that it still works. Sometimes one even "forgets" scanning is going on so that the repression becomes unconscious and takes more and more energy to reinforce—energy that might be used for growth. Such enforced blindness becomes destructive as a way of life and causes the winding down of the human spirit.

The next step in the process after the fundamental shift of energy is a working out of the primary images of the insight into language. We check with other people to see whether their experience and use of language have identified such an insight. The personal experience and "languaging" of the event become social. This checking ranges from the explicit language and formal rules of scientific investigation to insights that remain implicit in poetry and give rise to further images by which to explore the new frame of meaning.

Finally, there is a fifth step. After the opening, the scanning, the insight, and the articulation comes the will to closure. The closing tendency that began with the shift of energy could go on forever. We have all experienced an inability to bring closure to something we have been working on for a long time.

Even the scientist cannot always wait for all the data to be in. One can only work from one limited experiment to another, giving closure to each one. Finally, the will to closure must be exercised and closure accomplished.

When closure is accomplished, a new circle of meaning is completed. It can be used without thinking about how it was fashioned. Many gratefully forget the process by which the meaning was made because of the discomfort of such creative activity. Still, the new circle of meaning sits there, waiting to be broken by crisis or dissolved by wonder. The process will begin again, for it is the very stuff of life.

The fundamental process of the imagination is rooted in human nature. We seem born to create, always seeking a new frame for meaning that is broken or that we dissolve with wonder. More will be said about this in the next chapter.

The way for the teacher to support the creative process is to be aware of it. When the teacher is aware of the process and its pattern, then helping the child move with intention from the circle to an art or play response makes complete sense. This gets the process going. It also makes sense to allow children to wander around the room to see what material or lesson will speak to them, as long as their wandering is constructive. Opening and scanning are very important.

Closing and articulation are as important as opening and scanning. A child might be wandering to avoid the possibility of insight. A child who is making something for the teacher or for anyone else might be avoiding the move that takes him or her more deeply into the process of self-discovery. The creative process seems to need a deadline to shift from scanning to insight. Limits, therefore, are as important as being open. Teachers need to be aware of promoting both the opening and closing tendencies and should strive to balance them in individual children, in the group, and in their own lives.

The opening and closing of the creative process can also be the key to help us understand the worship-education styles of particular people. Teachers need to be careful not to project their own worship-education styles onto individual children. We need to be aware of these style differences and how they are connected to the creative process, so we can let people be who they are and help them move toward an integration of styles to enhance the carrying through of the whole creative process at all the levels of being human.

Supporting the Integration of Styles

Hippocrates was one of the first to divide humankind into types. About 450 B.C. he divided people into four temperaments. Typology has gone on ever since. Are you mercurial or jovial, introvert or extrovert, somatotonic-mesomorphic or ectomorphic-cerebrotonic, excitatory or inhibitory, tender-minded or tough-minded, reducer or augmenter, right-brained or left-brained?[3]

I will propose two pairs of opposing tendencies associated with the creative process. They are the opening and closing tendencies and the thinking and feeling tendencies. Feeling is more associated with scanning, and thinking is more associated with articulation. We are all of these tendencies, but one of each pair of opposing tendencies usually outweighs the other. The goal for the teacher is to support the whole process and to balance extreme tendencies by guiding the child toward developing the opposite tendency in each pair.

When worship tends toward thinking, the experience of explanation and understanding becomes of first importance. There is a great deal of thinking *about* God rather than entering into the language or experience of God. The sermon tends to give answers. The liturgy, sacred story, and parables are translated into generalizations to be thought about.

The kind of religious education that is related to thinking worship is also focused on explanation. The transfer of knowledge from one head to another is most important, and evaluation is based on the pupil's restating of what the teacher has said. The stories and poetry of the Bible are translated into concepts.

When feeling dominates, worship becomes primarily concerned with ecstatic fusion with the Holy and the community. Being in relationship with the self, others, God, and nature becomes the primary value. While the most valued part of the liturgy for thinking-tendency people is the sermon, the most important part of the liturgy for feeling-tendency people is the experience of God in Holy Communion. Similarly valued experiences include the classical conversion experience of confession-surrender-repentance, witnessing, and manifesting the "fruits of the spirit," such as by speaking in tongues.

The kind of religious education that is connected to the feeling tendency in worship is the winning of souls of the young and old who are not as yet one in the spirit or converted. What is taught is the fusion of feeling and will. People are also taught how to worship in order to achieve the fruits of the spirit when explicitly or implicity cued. The teaching of how to win souls by such experiencing is one of the most important goals of this kind of religious education.

While the thinking-tendency kind of worship seeks a certain distance in its relationships, the feeling-tendency worship seeks a closeness of relationship. Instead of thinking and debating there is sharing and a seeking of a warm consensus. This is true of both the worship and the corresponding religious education.

The other pair of opposing tendencies are the tendencies toward openness and closure. In worship tending toward openness, there is a sense of play and festival. This kind of worship is devoted to the search for truth and the pilgrimage of life. The dominating aspect of such worship is a sacramental system in which sacramental markers are used for life's stages and for pastoral care, but not in an exclusive way. There is a sense of inclusion of everyone and all of life.

The religious education tendency that is associated with the openness of worship is that of nurture and lifelong development. This kind of education emphasizes enculturation into how to use the sacramental system for marking life's changes and for pastoral care. The plurality of religious journeys is not only appreciated but also taught. There is an openness to the community in which one lives and serves. Evaluation is vague but growth-oriented.

Worship where the closure tendency dominates has a sense of duty and work about it. There are set channels through which God's grace flows, and there are set ways to practice the liturgy of using those channels. There is an emphasis on correct belief and the exclusion of those who do not use the liturgical system correctly.

The kind of religious education that fits this tendency in worship is one that teaches correct belief and the proper specific practice of life and worship. It is based on the authority of the perceived past. This kind of education attempts to conserve the truths that have been handed down. Evaluation is in terms of whether or not the answers that children, youth, or adults give are correct as measured by these ancient standards.

There is a tendency to set up a separate culture apart from the larger community. This "Christian" culture is clearly outlined with a system of "do's" and "don'ts" that enables insiders to exclude everyone who does not follow the prescribed path.

Each of these four tendencies of worship and religious education has both constructive and destructive elements. Some of the dangers illuminated by looking at the four tendencies in worship are very important. An exclusively closed tendency produces a tight, repressive, and over-controlling atmosphere in worship and religious education. On the other hand, an exclusively open tendency fosters an anxiety that develops from the freely flowing style of worship and religious education. Here there are no boundaries and no clarity of identity. Either extreme is destructive.

When a person or group becomes overly thinking in orientation, there is the danger that what can be known through feelings and intuition will atrophy. Distance and intellectualization will substitute for closeness and a personal awareness of God, the self, and one another.

Persons or groups that become overly feeling in orientation are also potentially destructive. Getting stuck in the extreme of feeling destroys the distance needed for perspective and the analytical ability to avoid being taken advantage of by unscrupulous religious leaders who seek only power, wealth, or control. The thinking tendency is needed to balance the potential loss of identity when the feeling tendency leads individuals to become merged with the group or lost in the fusion with the Holy. God seeks to set us free, not to make us slaves, but without the perspective, analysis, and distance of the thinking tendency, unreflective emotional intensity can make feeling-tendency people and groups, even those with the purest motives, into bigots and fanatics.

You may consider one or another of these descriptions of extremes to be artificially weighted either positively or negatively. They may be, but I have not intended them to be. This is, of course, a preliminary statement of these types, but there are two points about it that are especially important. First, I mean to value the flexibility and integration of these tendencies over getting stuck in one extreme position or another. Second, this typology provides a simple, and I hope not simplistic, way to guard against projecting our wishes onto the worship and educational styles of others.

I must hasten to say that sometimes it is important to be extreme. Sometimes the extreme position of another requires the firmness and clarity of the opposite tendency to counteract it. I am proposing, however, that we act from a centered, integrated, and flexible position rather than reacting in knee-jerk fashion to any stimulus that challenges our preferred style.

It is all very well to speak of "balancing" the four tendencies, but there are some individuals and groups who make a virtue of each of these extremes. Apart from this talk of balancing, is there any reason that shows the four tendencies to be of equal value? The answer to this question brings us to the joining of the creative process with these styles of knowing God.

One of the reasons I am convinced that the four tendencies are of equal value is that all four are needed to enable the full creative process to take place in the communication with God, self, others, and nature. To know the Creator in the creative process one needs openness, feeling, thinking, and closure at the right moment without getting stuck at any step in the process.

When disjunction takes place, the whole human system—biological, psychological, social, and spiritual—is involved to some degree. The deeper the involvement—in St. Paul's experience on the road to Damascus, for example—the more profound the transformation. The more profound the transformation, the more energy is shifted by the insight step toward the expression and elaboration steps. This is also illustrated by St. Paul, who spent the rest of his life communicating what he had discovered about the mystery of being "in Christ."

The openness tendency is needed during the scanning process to ensure that it can take place without being artificially blocked. For insight to take place we need not only openness but also feeling. This is because insight is usually intuited first in feelings, hunches, incomplete images, an other "unreasonable" events. The thinking tendency is needed for the expression and elaboration steps. The closure tendency is useful to promote the final closing of the meaning loop.

What is important for teachers about these tendencies is that they should be supported at the appropriate time in the process of discovery. For example, the feelings of discovery and the excitement of the breakthrough might be so attractive to a particular individual that he or she might stop at that step in the process and remain stuck in the feeling tendency.

The thinking tendency is needed to pull apart vagueness by analysis. When a person lacks the ability to apply the thinking tendency, or lacks the perspective needed to work with other types of people or groups on a team to compensate for one another's strengths and weaknesses, that individual will feel impotent, unable to contribute to life or to communicate who he or she is.

The inability to carry through this process of creation to completion will eventually break down anyone who is stuck in one of the tendencies. The image of God will become shattered and the wholeness of the person fragmented. This will give rise to the urge to destroy rather than create.

We all need one another to avoid getting stuck in one or the other of the tendencies in worship and thus frustrate the whole process of creativity of which we are a part. The *mysterion* of the mystic's openness needs the *sacramentum* of closure belonging to the institutional church. The philosophers and theologians among us need the charismatics. Those seeking fusional joy need the thinkers to lend distance and perspective. We all need one another in this system of relationships called the church, a body of many parts, needs, and gifts. We need one another to be the kind of creative creatures we are meant to be.

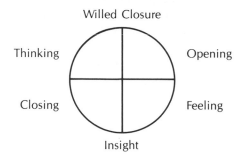

Søren Kierkegaard said in 1846 in his *Concluding Unscientific Postscript*[4] that to understand life one cannot oppose imagination and thinking or feeling. The task is not to exalt one aspect of knowing over another. It is to give all aspects of knowing equal status, for "they are unified in *existence.*" Joining the styles of knowing God with the process of knowing God unifies these important aspects of religious knowing, as Kierkegaard suggested they should be.

Supporting Stages and Stageless Knowing

The work of James Fowler needs little introduction.[5] He and his colleagues have identified the stuctures people use to give shape to their constructs of ultimate meaning. This form cannot be separated from what one has faith in, except for purposes of analysis. The sequence of these constructs develops in a consistent way from person to person, so one can make educated guesses about which particular faith stage another person might be using.

Tuning in the right meaning "channel" improves communication and reduces frustration. When we begin to use religious language, however, something curious happens. People seem to be able to participate in the same parable, sacred story, or liturgical act regardless of the Fowler stage they happen to be in. This language domain seems to involve a kind of language that is open to all stages. The trouble begins when people begin to talk *about* what the language is saying. That is when the cross-stage static can jam the communication.

Talking *about* what religious language is saying is different from being *in* the language. Being in the language, absorbed in meditation, is stageless.[6] The participant is not standing outside of himself or herself as an observer. There is no reflection of the coordinated action. Religious language acts as a door into the pure coordination of actions among God, self, others, and the creation. Being in religious language connects the imagination process to the coordination of actions. This being in the language is used in the first three steps of the creative process. As soon as one begins to articulate the new insight, Fowler's stages come into play. One becomes an observer again and begins to speak *about* religion.

Robert Kegan's studies of Piaget have called us to look past Piaget's stages to the movement that the stages mark. It is this movement that should be in the foreground while the stop-action descriptions are in the background. We should attend to "the constitutive activity rather than constitutions,"[7] or as Van Gogh said, he wanted to paint "not blossoms, but blooming." Kegan does not call the creating of meaning an act of the ego. His view is that this creating is done by the "creative motion of life itself." This process is philosophically real, biologically real, psychologically real, socially real, and religiously real. It is "the holy, the transcendent, and the oneness of all life."

In the classroom it is useful to use stages for matching faith channels for religious discussions. What is not so carefully attended to in these days of stage theories is the need to support stageless, more theological cognition.

Supporting Symbolic Activity

In 1978 Bruce Reed published his book *The Dynamics of Religion*[8] in England. The book covers many important dynamics, but "oscillation" between symbolic and work activity is one of the most fruitful for our purposes. A striking example of these two kinds of activity took place during the 1971 international Everest expedition. An Indian member was killed in an avalanche. The climbing party retreated below the snow line to burn the body, according to Hindu custom. When the ritual was completed, they returned to the place where the accident occurred and began to climb toward the summit again.

The climb down and back up was very difficult, and the hazard was great. The loss of time might mean that they would not be able to make the summit. Yet all the members of the team were convinced the climb down and back was worth doing. Why? It was a way to know that they inhabited a world of meaning rather than merely of natural facts over which they had no control. It created a sense of value of life and of their lives together. It was not work. It was symbolic. We human beings need such symbols.

Work is oriented toward dealing with present and future realities in the "public" and workaday world. Symbolic activity is a mental process involving symbols that connect with the world but originate in the imagination.

We must take charge of things to deal with the "public" world. When we worship, however, someone else is in charge. The clergy guide us through the liturgy of our tradition, and we have the chance to regress into a state of safety and dependence. This is a time to let the mind wander, daydream, and muse, to actively open the mind to be receptive to the Creator.

Many researchers in the social sciences have noticed the alternation of the human need for pushing forward and taking charge with the need for dreaming and playing. Winnicott,[9] for example, studied such regression to dependence. He found both a creative regression and a defensive regression. In creative regression we are able to let go of the habitual ways of seeing the world and ourselves that have gotten us stuck in a rut. The "observing ego" can remain unregressed and identified with the therapist or, perhaps, the clergy or worshiping community. When the old way is let go, a new way can begin to be imagined. You can see the pattern of the creative process at work in this transformation, and you can see the need of this kind of alternation for the creative process to find the stability and safety in which to make fundamental changes in one's view of the world and oneself.

Unfortunately, many in the church use worship to remain stuck in defensive regression. A false sense of security is established, and a wall is built up against change. In *The Concept of Dread*[10] Kierkegaard commented on the apparent peace and repose in this state. He goes on to say, however, that "there is nothing to strive with. What is it then? Nothing. But what effect does nothing produce? It begets dread. This is the profound secret of innocence, that at the same time it is dread." This is the impossible attempt of the adult to return to childhood. It is being childish and infantile rather than childlike.

Reed argued that teaching must be distinguished from worship and the sermon.[11] The sermon is for rehearsing the myths and evoking the symbolic ritual. The task of the teacher is to help the worshiper understand the language. Education, he said, should be carried out in nonworship settings. I agree to a point, but we cannot learn the art of using religious language well without actually using it appropriately. Consequently, the language needs to be used to communicate with God in worship. This is why Godly play is a combination of symbolic and work activity. As in worship, however, the symbolic aspect prevails.

Supporting Safety for the Open Mind

Safety and trust are important for the imagination and for symbolic activity. In his classic study of the open and closed mind, Milton Rokeach noted that belief/disbelief systems serve two powerful and conflicting sets of motives at the same time: the need for a cognitive framework in order to know and understand and the need to ward off threatening aspects of reality. He said, "A person will be open to information *insofar as possible*, and will reject it, screen it out, or alter it *insofar as necessary.*"[12]

The most troubling piece of this theory is that no matter how much a person's system closes up to ward off threat and anxiety, the subjective experience is no different from the way a person with an open mind experiences his or her frame of reference. The need to know is satisfied in either case. This is important to note both for the teacher's view of what is going on in the classroom as well as to know how to support the creative process by providing a safe place for it to do its work.

Three aspects of belief/disbelief systems were of special interest to Rokeach and his colleagues in their empirical studies.

They were the belief/disbelief continuum, the central/peripheral aspects of the systems, and the dimension of time perspective. All three are helpful to Godly play.

A person's system is open to the extent to which the person can receive, evaluate, and act on relevant information received from the outside on its own intrinsic merits, unencumbered by irrelevant factors arising from within the person or from the outside. Examples of irrelevant internal pressures are unrelated habits, beliefs, and perceptual cues, as well as irrational ego motives, power needs, the need for self-aggrandizement, or the need to allay anxiety. Irrelevant external pressures are those of reward and punishment arising from external authority such as that exerted by parents, peers, other authority figures, reference groups, or social, institutional, and cultural norms.

Someone with a closed belief system has difficulty distinguishing between information received about the world and information received about the source. Whether what the external source says is true is more important than evaluating the information on its own merits. Information from outside a closed system is accepted only if it comes through an authority important for maintaining that closed system.

The more closed the system, the more the world will be seen as threatening, the greater the belief in absolute authority will be, and therefore the more other persons will be evaluated according to the authorities they line up with. Flowing out of this mind-set is the attitude that the peripheral beliefs one holds are related to one another by virtue of their common origin in authority rather than by virtue of intrinsic connections. The closed person is forced to accept all or nothing as a "package deal."

The time perspective is also important. People with an open mind are rooted in the present. They make predictions and check them against future facts. They have little concern with the remote past or future, but use past, present, and future in a balanced way to evaluate present information. By contrast, close-minded people are most interested in the remote future, since it is impossible to refute. They can be safely preoccupied with it without disturbing present beliefs. Things that happen in the present are used to confirm the remote future.

The identification of the open and closed mind is important not only for estimating the safety of the environment for the imagination, but also for estimating which adults will be good teachers. A person with a closed mind is not likely to embody the active openness that the art of using religious language needs to be associated with or to support individuals and the group in the exploration of their own religious worlds.

Supporting the Theological Virtues and the Flow of Teaching

The Pauline emphasis on faith, hope, and love in the First Letter to the Corinthians (1.13) provides us with a guide to help analyze how the imagination can be approached theologically to avoid the limitations of the closed mind. This discussion of the function of the theological virtues in relation to the imagination needs to begin with a few words about virtues to dispel any lingering negative connotations about how the word *virtues* is being used here.

The English word *virtue* comes from the Latin *virtus.* This word signifies both strength and power (*vir*). When St. Thomas spoke of a virtue in the *Summa Theologiae* the connotation was broad, positive, and strong. A virtue implies the perfection of a power. It is the activity of a human power at its best. The virtuous person is not grim, stern, and overbearing, as is often inferred today. For St. Thomas the truly virtuous person enjoyed acting virtuously.

The four cardinal virtues are justice, fortitude, temperance, and prudence. Other qualities flow from these fundamental ones. The word *cardinal* comes from the Latin word *cardinalis,* which first meant "pertaining to a door-hinge." It implied something pivotal. Its meaning was later extended to include "that on which something depends."

The purpose of a virtue, as the term is used here, is to help us achieve happiness. Happiness is related to our nature and is attained through our natural capacities when they are well used. We are drawn to a higher kind of happiness, however. It is here that St. Thomas attempted to join Aristotle and scripture. We cannot attain Godly happiness through our human capacities alone. Our efforts need divine assistance. The theological virtues of faith, hope, and charity are infused in us by God.

What I wish to draw attention to here is not the intricate analysis of St. Thomas but his emphasis on faith, hope, and love as theological virtues. What I would like to say about these strengths is how important they are to the working of the imagination. To explore this importance, I would like to define faith, hope, and love by their opposites. I would like to oppose faith with anxiety, hope with despair, and love with hate. In each pairing of opposites the movement toward the theological virtue is related to being drawn into the pattern of the Creator's power.

Anxiety is a state of arousal that occurs when we perceive the presence of an unidentified threat. In this state we are prepared to stand and fight or to flee, but since no specific danger is apparent we're caught in the state of preparation. In time that sustained arousal can wear down the whole human system, biologically, psychologically, socially, and spiritually. Faith is the opposite. It is the state of not being anxious, and for no specific reason. In the state of faith we are stable, centered, alert, balanced, and prepared to deal both with specific fears and with nonspecific dangers with equilibrium.

Despair is a pervasive loss of expectation. Things are impossible. There is no way out. There is no single thing that is the focus of despair, as one might find in sadness about a loss. Despair is like "the pit" spoken of in many of the psalms. It is a pit without time and space. There is only doom. Hope is the opposite. It is open to the future. In hope there is expectation. Eager anticipation blooms. Instead of an empty pit there is a pervading sense of the possibility of fulfillment. There is a way out.

Hate destroys. It separates. It drives people apart. It moves people against one another. It takes advantage of people. It destroys creating in others. Love creates. It creates families and children. It creates relationships. Love moves people toward one another. It builds people up. It helps create creating in others.

The theological virtues are positive powers. It is not enough to refrain from the states of anxiety, despair, and hate.

It is not enough to refrain from acts stemming from such states. Movement toward the other end of these continua is the only way to resist a life of action grounded in anxiety, despair, or hate. The dangerous thing is that when one of these states begins to dominate, it can carry one or both of the other two with it.

Movement toward hate, despair, and anxiety is movement toward a closed mind. A closed mind leads us toward being a closed system, one that is winding down. The potential is used up. We become empty. Movement toward faith, hope, and love is movement toward the renewing of energy through the imagination in an open system, so there is always new potentiality rather than the using up of a limited quantity of energy in a closed system.

Faith, hope, and love are very much involved with the imagination. Faith is the safe place in which one can live to take the risks of the imagination's discoveries. Hope is the open door, held open for the new to come in. Love is the movement toward the unknown as it comes to meet us through the open doorway.

Faith, hope, and love make a circle that reinforces itself. The creative process, however, uses particular strengths for its different tasks. Hope is what helps us open the door with wonder. Love creates the image with the Spirit that is drawn out into language. Faith comes as the process draws to a conclusion and gives us the ability to bring about closure by an act of the will. We need to support all three theological virtues in a classroom where there is Godly play.

Kierkegaard wrote in his *Journals:* "Imagination is used by Providence to draw men toward reality, toward existence and to lead them far, deep, or low enough into existence. And when imagination has helped them to go as far as they can, that is precisely where reality begins."[13] With this thought in mind, we turn to the next chapter. There we will take a deeper look at what the imagination is. Much has been assumed up to this point. It is now time to become more explicit.

6 The Imagination and Godly Play

Getting involved with the imagination is always dangerous. It draws us into change. Seeing the world in a different way can change us as well as the world. Will the imagination also detach us from reality and trap us in a world of fantasy? There is a positive and a negative side to the imagination—and yet can life be "imagined" without it?

THE ORIGIN OF THE IMAGINATION

Evidence of people's wondering about the imagination can be found at the very beginnings of Western civilization. The Jews and the Greeks explored the ambiguity of imagination in their writings about ultimate origins. Later, Christians explored how Christ and the imagination fit together. To better understand the imagination and its relation to Godly play, we need to begin at the beginning with the theft of fruit and fire.

About 950 B.C., during the period of the Unified Kingdom under Solomon, the Yahwistic tradition of Genesis was written and edited. This included the second creation story (Genesis 2.4b–2.5) as well as the Fall (3.1–7) and Adam's theft of the fruit. In Greece about 800 B.C. Hesiod's *Theogony* was written. It included the story of Prometheus (pro-metheus, fore-sight) and the theft of fire.

The priestly tradition of Genesis was put into writing after the Exile, sometime during the period of about 538–450 B.C.[1] The priests put existing literary traditions and some new material into their own framework. The first creation story (Genesis 1.1–2.4a) was added, and it established the context for the more ancient second story. In Greece, the founder of Greek drama, Aeschylus (525–455 B.C.), devoted three of his ninety or so plays to Prometheus. Only *Prometheus Bound* has survived.

In both Genesis traditions God created the earth alone. The creation of the imagination, however, was completely different. God was not able to do this alone. To create the imagination took clay into which life had already been breathed. It took companions, Adam and Eve. It took the serpent to suggest the unthinkable. It took the tree with the fruit that Adam and Eve were not to touch. It took a risk. Creatures who can create can also destroy! To create the imagination, God had to say no.

In Eden we existed in dreaming innocence, naming things and exercising dominion. God said no, and our forebears stole the fruit. The mirror of language came into being at the same time and showed us that we were naked. Our eyes were opened. We created culture to clothe ourselves. When God said no, the negation implied freedom and created a kind of creature who could create.

Prometheus was one of the Titans. His brother, Epimetheus (epi-metheus, afterthought), was inclined to follow his first impulse and then change his mind. He had a hand in the Greek creation. By the time Epimetheus got around to making people, the best gifts had already been given away—strength, swiftness, fur, feathers, wings, shells, and so on. He asked his brother for help. Prometheus first fashioned a creature who walked upright like the gods. He then went to the sun and brought back fire, which was an even better protection than the animals had. This and other things Prometheus had done so angered Zeus that he had Prometheus chained to a high, sharp rock. The messenger, Hermes, was sent to warn him that if he did not make his peace with Zeus his body would be torn to rags all the day long and an eagle, red with blood, would feast on his blackened liver in fury.

Both the Jews and the Greeks considered the imagination to be dangerous. The fire of Prometheus might help people cope with nature, but it can also burn human beings. Humankind can become so inflamed by its power that the resulting pride can burn out the human spirit to ashen emptiness. Only tragedy can result.

Adam freely chose to steal the fruit. After the Fall Adam and Eve could not go back, but they could go forward. There was no redemption for Prometheus, except in a later tradition involving Charon, but Prometheus sought no pardon and stoically lived out his cosmic destiny. He maintained his identity by defiance of Zeus. The identity of Adam and Eve was also worked out in relation to God, but their sense of self included the possibility of redemption.

Two Jewish traditions developed to interpret the imagination.[2] The Hebraic imagination was seen by the Torah as a transgression to be bound and suppressed. Imagination was thought to be an evil impulse. It caused us to be cut off from the immediacy of the moment with God, and it continues to do so.

In the Talmud the way of suppression was replaced with the way of integration. The Talmud views imagination as part of God's plan. There is a good aspect to the imagination as well as a dangerous and evil one. The good imagination enables us to participate in an I-Thou dialogue with our Creator and to help fulfill the purpose of the Holy One.

There is a Midrash (*Genesis Rabba*, 12) that evokes the fundamental dilemma in the nature of humankind. If God formed people from the elements of the superior world, there would be no peace, because the superior spirit would overcome the earthly. If God formed humankind only from the earth, there would be no peace either. The earthly would constantly threaten the spiritual. God, therefore, created humankind from both elements at once, dust and spirit.

The Greeks also had two great traditions about the imagination. Plato (428–348 B.C.) condemned the imagination as a mirror. In Book 10 of the *Republic* Plato made five primary accusations against the imagination. All were related to his view that the imagination is only mimetic. It does not give true knowledge.

Plato did acknowledge that images could be used to aid understanding. A mathematician might use a drawing of a square to help pupils comprehend the invisible square in the mind. In addition Plato hinted that there was a special kind of knowledge that the imagination could disclose.

In the somewhat mystical dialogues, particularly in the *Phaedrus* and the *Timaeus,* Plato spoke of visionary images given to chosen people to show them what the soul could not ordinarily perceive in daylight. He also wrote about inspired images that arise in the sleep of seers. Plato located this function in the liver, the part of the body that the eagle of Zeus picked at daily to punish Prometheus.

A completely different view of the imagination is presented in the writings of Aristotle (384–322 B.C.). His discussion turned from metaphysics and gods to human psychology. The imagination's function is to provide a mental intermediary between sensation and reason. The image serves as a bridge between inner and outer experience. Without the transitional role of the imagination, reason would be unable to make contact with the sensible world of reality. Thought without images would be empty. The mediation of the imagination's mental images gives us the possibility of reason.

In the Christian view, Jesus is the creative act incarnate in a life. That life is known through four narratives, the Gospels. We are creatures of time and space, so we need narratives in time and space to better understand our own nature. The incarnation of the Logos is the story in which we find our story.

Christ became the visible image of the invisible God of Genesis. Christ stimulates our imagination to know the God no one has ever seen by restoring God's image, which we had at the beginning but lost in the Fall. For centuries this image was thought of as some kind of substance, but during the sixteenth-century Reformation it came to be understood as a relationship. Today the point of contact might be thought of as the overlapping processes of the creative spirit in Creator and creature.[3]

The ancient stories of origin and their interpretation provide us with an astounding view of human nature. We are an unstable mixture of spirit and clay. Neither heaven nor earth can dominate without destroying the other part of who we are. We are an ambiguity. Our very structure renders the imagination ambiguous.

What, then, does the imagination do? What is the outline of its function?

THE FUNCTIONAL SHAPE OF
THE IMAGINATION

Philosophers have been interested in the logical analysis of the imagination for thousands of years. Their analysis of the imagination broke it up into significant parts. The next step was to pit one significant part against another to suggest the key to the imagination's functioning. These positions are still present in today's discussions about the imagination.

Rather than debating the various positions it is more useful to make a map of the discussion's tendencies to see what can be revealed about it as a whole. Paul Ricoeur, the influential French philosopher associated with the University of Paris and the University of Chicago, made such a map in 1986 to picture the problematic and equivocal nature of the imagination in Western philosophy.[4]

We will look, first, at the degrees of difference among philosophers along one line of definition, the origin of the image. Let us call that the horizontal axis of the discussion. The vertical axis of the discussion involves the degrees of difference about a person's depth of involvement with the image.

At the extreme left of the horizontal line, the image is defined as the trace of a perception. It is a weakened impression that reproduces objects in the external world. Ricoeur suggested the example of Hume. At the other extreme, the far right of the horizontal line, is a position like that of Sartre. The imagination is thought to create the presence of an image without any stimulus from the outside. The definition of the imagination running along the horizontal line, then, moves between the two extremes from the reproduction of images to the production of images by the imagination.

The vertical line of the philosophical discussion is concerned with the one who imagines. At the top of this line is a kind of absorbing fascination with images that confuses the real with the imaginary. Ricoeur suggested Pascal and Spinoza as examples. At the bottom of the line is the person who keeps a critical distance from the image so that the imagination can function as an instrument for the critique of reality. Husserl is the example Ricoeur proposed.

One should be able to locate any major logical or historical position on this map of four philosophical tendencies. The point is that the imagination is defined in different ways and the whole map needs to be taken into consideration to truly understand what the imagination is. It has a variety of uses, so a variety of definitions are needed to contain its full meaning.

Mary Warnock tracked the philosophical view of the imagination from Hume through Kant to Coleridge and Wordsworth, and on into the twentieth century by way of phenomenology to Wittgenstein, Ryle, and Sartre, to see what conceptual connections there might be among these many and different philosophers.[5] She concluded that meanings spring up around us as soon as we are conscious. It is the imagination that visualizes these meanings in the objects about us, from the "ordinary three-dimensional furniture of the world" to the diagrams in a book. Her picture of the imagination's function is a circular one, like a feedback loop. It moves from rendering the world familiar and therefore manageable to rendering our experience unfamiliar and mysterious. It then renders things manageable again, and so on.

Warnock proposed that if our imagination is at work "tidying up the chaos of sense experience" it is also at work on yet another level to make it untidy again. The imagination is a power, then, that combines a sense of chaos-making and order-making. It gives value to the world by revealing that there is always more, and it yet suggests the possibility of adequate control. Somehow the imagination reduces what is too expansive and expands what has been reduced to oversimplification. The imagination keeps us alive through its ambiguous power.

Philosophers, of course, use the imagination to construct their views about how the imagination functions. The interest of painters and other artists is slightly different. They want to know how to use the imagination to practice their craft, not to know it in itself. In addition artists are especially interested in the connection between their images and the reality they intend to disclose by their art.

THE ARTIST AND THE IMAGINATION

Richard Kearney's book *The Wake of Imagination*[6] is concerned with images and the imagination in art. He has confronted the so-called postmodern obsession with the demise of the imagination. He probed deeply into the history of the imagination to begin to imagine what the view of the imagination will be like in the future.

To organize the fundamental views of art and reality presented by Kearney, we will use the image of a triptych. It is a three-paneled piece of art, made from wood, with a painting on each of the panels. Let's open up the triptych and begin to look from left to right at the faces painted there. Imagine the faces that Richard Kearney used in his book. They are Christ the Pantocrator, the last self-portrait of Van Gogh, and a poster of an exploding Van Gogh by Martin Sharp. These portraits represent the premodern, modern, and postmodern views of the imagination and reality.

Premodern: Christ the Pantocrator (Creator of All)

The artist of Jerusalem or Athens was primarily a craftsman. The potter making a pot made a work of art, but the pot was also useful in everyday life. Artistic activity was modeled on the divine creator, or the Platonic *demiourgos*. The Christian synthesis of Hebrew and Greek views in the medieval period saw the icon maker, the cathedral master builder, the painter, the scribe, and others serving and following the transcendent plan of the Creator in their work.

The artist of the Middle Ages was usually unknown. The point of creating the art was not to call attention to the artist but to serve God. An icon like the face of Christ was never signed. Nor could anonymous works be identified by any individual's style. The goldleaf background, the stylized features, the expressionless eyes were all formally set. The art and the artist were not to intrude on the purpose of the art, which was to guide the viewer's vision to the ultimate reality of God.

A medieval painting was a sacrament. The eyes often have no vanishing point in the painting. They do not look back at the viewer, nor do they seem to limit the space or time in the icon. One looks through the vanishing point into the mystery of God. The nonpictorial space around the face is rendered without perspective, so the figures are weightless. They are in the same plane, so there is no sense of movement to suggest time or the space in which such movement might take place.

Modern: Van Gogh, Self-Portrait

Since the Renaissance, art has shifted from a theocentric emphasis to an anthropocentric one. Van Gogh's picture of himself moved the mirror in front of the artist and is itself the reflection of the artist. The image, however, is not a mirrored reflection of the surface reality of the artist or the world. It is an expression of resounding originality. The artist's style and colors are like an autograph. They call attention to themselves. Art has become self-expression, even when there is little left to express but one's own despair. Art as a mirror of God's revelation has become art as a burning candle flame of self-revelation. In a way Christ, the martyr, has been replaced by Van Gogh, the martyr, who sacrificed himself for art and truth.

The artist in the modern age was an inventor. The age ushered in many kinds of explorers, from the navigators who sailed the seas to discover new worlds, to those who experimented in science, to those who engineered iron bridges, steam engines, and other marvels. Whereas the premodern period had prevailed on the artist not to put beauty between the observer and God, this period created the beauty of the painting as a means in itself to reveal reality.

Postmodern: Martin Sharp's Pop Poster of Van Gogh

The shift from theocentric to anthropocentric comes to rest in this face as the excentric paradigm of parody. Neither God nor the artist is central to the art. The images are moved about on the surface of the picture without asking for much more in the way of reality. These images don't refer to God or humankind so much as to one another.

Martin Sharp's picture explodes the contained madness of Van Gogh's original self-portrait into a psychedelic orgy of multiple reproductions. There are cut-out reproductions of pictures to create an image such as Van Gogh painting his own portrait. The images are reversed, superimposed, and distorted. In a yellow, comic-strip balloon the viewer can read: "I have a terrible lucidity at moments, when nature is so glorious in those days I am hardly conscious of myself and the picture comes to me like a dream."[7] Are these words of Van Gogh a meaningful self-revelation to be taken seriously, or is this word balloon a burlesque of the whole way he made meaning with images and the imagination?

A repulsive, huge, photo-realistic eye breaks out of the center of the poster like a balloon about to burst. Does it refer to the insanity in Van Gogh's eyes, or does it point to his single vision? Does it represent the eye of the artist's mind? Is it meant to be only a trick of technique? Perhaps the picture says that there is no meaning here at all and that the viewer is naive to imagine there is.

The postmodern artist arranges fragments of other people's art. The imagination is an electronic image-maker. Fragments of meaning are toyed with, but they do not seem to point anywhere outside the picture. The imagination of the postmodern period can at best parody, simulate, or reproduce. The mirror of God and the mirror of the self are replaced by a labyrinth of mirrors. Art is a light show, made up of floating signifiers without reference or reason except to reflect among their own reflections.

Postmodern artists seem weary and wary. They are uncertain about art's role in universal meaning. They question their ability to shape political events or to illuminate the identity of a human subject. This is why the question has been raised about whether the imagination is about to die.

When we go to museums, all three kinds of art are often present. There seems to be no way to link them together into a single frame. They are paradigms. We must leave them in their own worlds, framed in their own frames. Or must we?

We have discussed the philosophical inquiry about the imagination as if it were a two-dimensional map. We have also pictured the contribution of the artist in a triptych. It is now time to use yet another perspective. Let's look at the discussion about the imagination as if it were a three-leveled conversation and phenomenon.

THE "LEVELS" OF THE IMAGINATION

We seldom think about it, but as human beings we are conscious of a limited range of sounds. If we have the ear and the training for music, we can identify certain collections of sounds as music rather than noise. We can even write down the notes so that others can repeat the association of sounds by singing them or by playing them on a musical instrument. When the music is played or sung, it can be listened to and interpreted to be a love song, a setting for the mass, or some other kind of music that evokes certain kinds of emotions. There are three levels of imagination at work simultaneously in these events.

The discussion of the imagination can get terribly muddled if the three levels of interpretation are confused. The first level admits into our experience what the sensory apparatus of the human being can take note of (such as a range of sounds). The second level of the imagination selects certain bits from the sensory data of human experiencing for special recognition (music). This is perception. The third level of the imagination gives meaning to what has been selected by perception as a particular kind of perception (the mass).

To begin with the most basic level, what are the fundamental categories by which human beings experience life? Answers to this question are assumed in the analysis of the second level of perception, where experience "makes sense." The perception level and the level of fundamental categories are both assumed in the analysis of the third level, the meaning level.

Historically it has been the philosophers who have been most interested in sorting out the fundamental categories by which human beings experience life. Today, however, a combination of philosophical and scientific training better equips one to cope with this kind of question. Empirical research has opened up conversations between biology and behavior, between behavior and genetics, and among the comparative studies of animal behavior.

We might call the fundamental categories by which we experience life the "biological constraints on the human spirit." This is the phrase Melvin Konner used as the subtitle to his elegant book *The Tangled Wing*.[8] This book is an especially readable example of what is needed in addition to philosophy to cope with this level of questions about the imagination. Konner's particular training was in biology and anthropology at Harvard, a background he continued broadening in medical school.

Some philosophers who have spoken about the nature of humankind have seemed determined to speak without careful observation of the facts. Hobbes (1588–1679), the English philosopher of resignation, derived his philosophy from a view of the "nasty" natural state, whereas Rousseau (1712–1778), the Swiss-born philosopher of the golden natural state, said society was the root of all evil. Today we have access to so many studies of biology and anthropology that a philosopher could hardly be taken seriously who was not knowledgeable about these databases.

There is another kind of philosophy, however, that attempts to use the mind to know the mind. A classic example is the thought of Immanuel Kant (1724–1804). Kant initiated what he called a "Copernican revolution" in philosophy. Instead of explaining concepts by experience, as Hume and the British empiricists had done, he explained experience by concepts. He identified logically the human limit system. The system involves the fundamental intuitions of space and time as well as four categories or structures by which anything we experience comes to our attention. The categories he identified are quantity (unity, plurality, and totality), quality (reality, negation, and limitation), relation (substance and accident, causality and dependence, and interaction), and modality (possibility/impossibility, existence/nonexistence, and necessity/contingency).

At this level of inquiry the imagination is not related to any part or aspect of experience, but to experience itself. It selects, integrates, and mediates the sensory preconditions of our experience. It does not deal with the "content" of our experience. It deals with the possibility of there being any experience at all.

The analysis of the imagination at the next level, as perception, takes for granted the fundamental categories that establish experience. Both philosophers and psychologists have been interested in this level of discussion. Do we experience things as unified patterns, as the Gestalt psychologists argue we do? Or do we build up our perceptions by adding bits of atomistic sense data into a cumulative association, as the behaviorists argue? Such questions about perception are related to the role of the imagination in thinking, knowing, and interpreting experience.

The third level is the level that primarily interested Garrett Green in his book *Imagining God: Theology and the Religious Imagination.*[9] This level of thinking about the imagination takes for granted the presuppositions of the two prior levels. Inquiry at this level discusses the imagination as the process of interpretation itself. All kinds of interpretation, from the natural sciences to the humanities and social sciences, are included.

At this level the subject matter is not available to direct observation. It is mediated by selective and integrating images. These images come from our experience of the world that is immediately accessible, the "mesocosmic" world of every day. The microcosmic and macrocosmic worlds are invisible to us without technology such as microscopes and telescopes to examine them.

The fundamental ambiguity of the imagination appears at this level. The imagination can represent anything not directly accessible, including both the imaginary world and what we agree is the "real" world. It is the medium of fiction as well as fact. The use of the imagination at this level depends on larger frameworks of meaning, from the normative texts of the biblical canon to the latest model for the atom. Such frameworks help us imagine the world of science, religion, law, and other language domains by which we live. In fact, it seems that without the imagination we might not be able to live.

THE NECESSITY OF THE IMAGINATION

A chimera is an imaginary beast. During the Middle Ages a great deal of curiosity and delight was aroused by depictions of unique animals formed from the parts of various real animals. The chimera usually had a lion's head, a goat's body, and a serpent's tail. Such an image is a foolish fancy. It is the imagination gone wrong. On the other hand, it is delightful precisely because it is impossible except in the imagination.

Robert W. Weisberg[10] is an experimental psychologist and professional chimera hunter. He has devoted his life to the careful testing of theories about creativity. He has been hunting down imaginary images of the creative process to do away with them and so clear the field for a theory of the creative process based on fact rather than folklore.

The view of the imagination that Weisberg has arrived at is midway between the two extremes of the genius view and the "nothing new" view. The genius view of imagination includes the related ideas of unconscious thought processes, far-ranging leaps of insight, unique personal characteristics, and some indefinable quality. The nothing-new view can be traced back to John Watson, one of the pioneers in the development of behaviorism in the United States. This position suggested that we generalize from past experience about a similar situation in the present to arrive at a creative solution. If the new situation does not connect in any way with our past experience, then we behave randomly, combining various responses in all sorts of ways until we accidentally arrive at something acceptable.

Weisberg's position is that the creative process is neither so mysterious as the genius view implies nor so trivial as the behaviorist claims. His position is based on the result of controlled experiments and the careful study of reports about creativity made not only by artists, scientists, and inventors but also by ordinary people.

The definition of creativity that Weisberg uses has two parts. The first part is the novel response to a given situation. A creative solution is more than a repetition of some old solution. Novelty, however, is not enough. The second part of the definition is that the response must solve the problem at hand. The new idea must also work.

Careful empirical research takes patience. Most of the time it only rules out error, but this is positive. It helps to cast doubt on intuition or received opinion in order to clear the way for a new and more adequate theory. Karl Duncker's "candle problem" is an example of the kinds of experiments on which empirical research on the creative process is based.

Duncker's candle problem has been studied by psychologists for almost fifty years. A person is given a candle, a box of tacks, and a book of matches. The subject is then seated before a three-sided box sitting on a table. The experimenter instructs the subject to attach the candle to the *side* of the box so that there can be light for reading.

Confronted with this novel problem, most people set about manipulating the candle and tacks in various ways. Melted wax won't work to hold the candle to the side of the box. Sticking the tacks through the box into the candle won't work. The only way to solve the problem neatly is to melt the wax and stick the candle upright in the tack box. This box is then attached with tacks to the side of the larger box. The candle can now be lighted, and the smaller box even catches the wax as it burns.

Thinking aloud does not change the way the problem is treated, so the researcher records the stream of consciousness verbalized during study. The results show that people try out approaches based on past experience first. They then modify their solutions to meet the problems the new situation confronts them with. This in turn provides new information and by small steps a solution is reached that solves the problem.

This experience suggests a very simple explanation of the creative process. It works by applying past experience. New ideas are generated bit by bit. Everyone seems to be able to solve problems in this way. However, there are three traditional explanations of creativity that seem to argue against this single and simple one.

One of the traditional explanations is that creativity is arrived at by "leaps" of insight. No special knowledge is needed for such a flash of spontaneous restructuring. A second tradition is that there are two kinds of thinking. One works by free association, like Freud's primary process. The other kind of thinking uses logic to arrive at conclusions. The third tradition is that there is something special about creative people. We will look at these explanations in turn and, with Weisberg, do a little chimera hunting ourselves.

The "Leap of Insight" Chimera

Experiments like the candle problem have clarified various aspects of the creative process. For example, doubt has been cast on the theory that new combinations of ideas are brought about in the unconscious. In 1926 Graham Wallas[11] proposed a four-step creative process. The first stage is preparation, which involves a long period of conscious work without success. The second stage is incubation. This is a period of rest. The third stage is illumination, when the new idea is born. The last stage is verification.

It is during incubation that the work of the unconscious is supposed to take place. There are, however, other explanations for why taking a break is useful in generating a solution. During such an interlude one becomes more flexible and relaxed. Perspective is gained. A new set or angle of attack on the problem is noticed while one continues to worry about the problem during the break. Neither a theory of the unconscious nor one of solutions without stimuli is needed to explain such a breakthrough.

The spontaneous leap of insight was also discussed by the Gestalt psychologists. They thought that it came from a form of perception. This story began in the early twentieth century when associationism was the dominant psychological force. Associationist psychologists thought that solving a new problem depends on the transfer of associations from old situations to the new situation. The Gestalt psychologists argued against this view by saying that what they called productive thinking goes beyond one's past experience. Reproductive solutions are based on memory, but productive solutions are based on perception.

Gestaltists illustrated the power of perception by using ambiguous figures that shift as a whole before one's eyes. One such figure shifts back and forth from a rabbit to a duck. Confronted with another such figure, the Necker cube, the viewer shifts from seeing the depth in the cube to seeing the cube projecting out toward the viewer.

The Gestalt psychologists' explanation is relatively easy to test. Consider, for instance, the famous nine-dot problem. It is made up of three groups of three dots arranged on a page to form a square. The instructions are to connect all nine dots with four straight lines without lifting your pencil from the paper. The problem cannot be solved as long as you try to stay within the area delineated by the rows of dots. The assumption of the Gestalt psychologists was that once the outline of the nine dots is broken as a limit to the problem the answer should appear visually as a whole, as a new figure does in the shifting-figure diagrams.

This does not happen. Try it. Even though you know in advance that the solution can only be discovered by going outside the square formed by the nine dots, the answer does not flash before your eyes. You still need to work out the answer by trying different approaches. Multiple restructurings are required.

It is also clear that it takes more than a visual flash of perception to find solutions to most problems. It takes specific knowledge about the problem. Edward Thorndike's experiments with cats demonstrated this point. The cats were placed in novel situations in which they needed to solve a problem to get food. Solutions were acts such as pulling a string to open a door or pushing aside a vertical pole. Thorndike found that the animals only very gradually learned what they had to do to get out of the cage to get the food. They showed no "intelligence" or "reasoning ability." They used trial and error until they acquired the relevant experience so they could respond in an appropriate way.

Wolfgang Köhler, a leader of the Gestalt movement, spent World War I on the island of Tenerife, where he studied problem solving among apes. He laid all the parts of the problem in front of the ape, so that the ape could put the problem and solution together visually. The elements of the problem included such things as a stick to rake food into reach from inside the cage, or boxes placed inside the cage, where they could be piled up to reach a banana hanging from the ceiling. Köhler's apes were observed to produce novel solutions to such problems without any directly relevant past experience, seemingly lending support to the "flash of insight" view.

The flash of insight Köhler's apes experienced was tested by Herbert Birch in the 1970s. Köhler's apes had been captured from the wild, but Birch's five apes were raised from birth in captivity. None of these apes was able to put together the solution to problems as Köhler's apes had done, despite having all of the elements visually present. This suggests that there was some past learning that enabled Köhler's apes, raised naturally in the wild, to put together the puzzles he posed for them.

The gap between Thorndike's trial-and-error results and Köhler's insightful-animals approach was bridged by Harry Harlow in the late 1940s. He gave his apes a long series of more than three hundred discrimination problems. To obtain a food reward, the ape had to choose between two objects, such as a ball and a cross, set in front of the cage. When each new problem was presented, the animal first picked one of the two stimuli at random, since it could not know which stimulus hid the food. Once the first choice was made, however, the animal never made a mistake. If the first choice was incorrect, the animal picked the other stimulus and never returned to the incorrect one. At the end of the series one might say that the animal had "learned" how to solve the problems without fumbling. Harlow called this ability a "learning set."

The leap of insight is a chimera, because a careful look shows that animals and people learn by small steps when they are solving problems. We turn now to another chimera, the idea that there are special people born with creativity.

The "Gifted Genius" Chimera

The idea of the gifted genius is deeply embedded in our culture. Some folk tales associate creativity with madness. Another classical tradition refers to ancient Greece and the nine daughters of Zeus, the Muses, who ruled the arts and sciences. The Muses breathed creative ideas into the genius. Our word *inspiration* even comes from the Latin for "breathe in."

Today our culture is not as interested in speaking of God, the gods, or madness as it is in seeing whether we can identify the quality of genius by isolating specific characteristics in creative individuals. If that could be done, then the creative potential of a child could be assessed. Education for creativity could be established, and child rearing could be related to creativity.

The result would be an increase in creativity in the general population.

One of the problems with the dream of studying creative people is that of definition. Unfortunately, no specific characteristics have emerged to distinguish creative people from ordinary people in particular professions, except, perhaps, the drive to make more money or achieve other standards of success. Even if such characteristics could be identified, there is still the problem that such a correlational study would not tell us whether the particular characteristic or set of characteristics *caused* the creativity. For example, being self-directed might make one more creative, but being creative might also make one more self-directed.

Even if one assumes that there is a causal relationship between a certain personality trait and creativity, there is no uniform evidence that creativity is a constant in the life of the person judged to be a genius. Leonardo da Vinci, for example, is famous for his original thinking, but some of his creative thoughts were mistakes. We tend to forget his flying machine that was supposed to fly by flapping its wings or his new method for painting on plaster that caused his *Last Supper* in Milan to fade prematurely.

The definition of the creative genius also has a cultural dimension. Take J. S. Bach, for example. When he died in 1750, the public performance of his works died with him. His genius was not recognized for about seventy-five years. Genius is not a characteristic like eye color.

In the early Bach revival the fact that Bach was a German was probably more important than the quality of his music. Germany had suffered military and political humiliations during the Napoleonic period. Bach gave the German people a musical genius, a kind of offsetting victory. The response of the audience—whatever that response may be based on—is of great importance to the definition of an individual as a creative genius.

The "Two Kinds of Thinking" Chimera

Sputnik I was launched in October of 1957. This event not only ushered in the space age but also marked the first time in nearly forty years that the technological supremacy of the United States had been challenged by a powerful adversary. American scientific education was questioned, and so was our creativity.

In 1941 there was no mention of "creativity" in the *Encyclopedia of Educational Research*. In 1950 the heading "creative" was included in a list of higher mental processes, but without further elaboration. In 1960 "creative thinking" appeared as a brief subsection of the article on higher mental processes. In the fourth edition of 1969 "creativity" was given the status of its own independent article.[12]

In his presidential address to the American Psychological Association in 1950, James P. Guilford observed that in the preceding two decades there had appeared only 186 books or articles on creativity. By 1965 *Psychological Abstracts* listed 132 items published during that one year alone! The creative process and creativity have become popular subjects of inquiry in the latter half of this century.

In addition to psychologists and educational psychologists there was another group struggling to understand creativity. This was the group interested in teaching creativity. This approach assumed that we could all be taught to be creative, so the theory of the genius with special characteristics was assumed to be incorrect. During the early 1950s Alex Osborn produced books, speeches, and seminars with a patriotic fervor that now seems old-fashioned. It was Osborn who developed the term and method for "brainstorming."

Osborn proposed that there are two kinds of thinking: judicial and creative. We are each born with creative capacity, but this ability often fades over the years. Judgment takes over. Sometimes premature judgment can interfere with creativity. It causes us to reject as incorrect ideas that might solve the problem if given more of a chance to be worked out.

Osborn advanced a method for fostering creativity and used the number of new ideas produced as evidence for the method's success. The method included group brainstorming, the ruling out of criticism, the encouragement of freewheeling, the development of more and more new ideas, and the combination and improvement of ideas by others in the group.

The Gestalt psychologists had demonstrated the negative effects of fixation on past experience. The "Aha!," they said, comes when one breaks away from what has already been done. This conclusion seemed to support the emphasis on generating new ideas, and it established the assumption that the more ideas produced about a problem, the better.

Indeed, the number of new ideas generated in Osborn's brainstorming sessions was impressive. What was not impressive was the number of new ideas that actually solved problems. It was about the same number as was produced by groups that came up with fewer ideas overall. In addition, little difference could be shown between working alone and working with others in a brainstorming group.

When divergent or free-form thinking itself dominated the definition of creativity, the generation of new ideas was detached from the generation of solutions that actually solved problems. Creativity tests and teaching methods in turn were narrowed to fit this view and its truncated definition of creativity.

At mid-century Guilford spoke of divergent and convergent thinking. Edward De Bono, a leader in the creativity training movement today, speaks of lateral and vertical thinking. Vertical thinking digs the hole deeper. Lateral thinking spreads out and generates new viewpoints. William Gordon has used the Greek word *synectics* to refer to the joining together of different and apparently irrelevant elements in a problem. James Adams, like many of the creativity teachers, has spoken of how to dissolve "blocks" to one's use of the divergent, lateral, or synectic kinds of thinking needed to produce new ideas.

According to Adams, perceptual expectations are one kind of block that can interfere with creativity. One can artificially narrow the problem. Another block is to look at the problem from only one viewpoint. Some people block their creativity by fearing to take a risk. Others are afraid they will appear foolish. Judging is safer than producing a new idea and testing it. Sometimes a lack of cooperation from one's co-workers blocks the creative process. Also, our culture tends to emphasize the linear, logical approach. A struggle to be too efficient can squash creativity, because "fooling around" is needed to generate new ideas. Some people have a hard time expressing ideas during a problem-solving session. Adams has shown how his "blockbusting" can release creative thinking by dissolving some of these obstacles.

Such work has produced useful results, but its value does not depend on there being two distinct kinds of thinking. In fact, there is little evidence that creativity is a special kind of thinking. Careful research shows that creative thinking is not extraordinary. It becomes extraordinary because of what is produced, not because of the way the innovative solution was produced.

Group problem solving turns out to be less productive than that of individuals, and brainstorming instructions are less effective than instructions that emphasize initial criteria and judgment. Studies also indicate that creative scientific thinking is not related to divergent thinking ability.

Finally, there is a basic misunderstanding about the logic of divergent thinking. The fresh viewpoint supposedly turned up by divergent thinking could be borrowed from another person to whom it was not fresh. This is an example of borrowing another person's work and experience rather than creativity.

The fundamental point of Weisberg's chimera hunting is the discovery that there is nothing fundamentally extraordinary about creative people. We all possess the basic capacities that allow us to adapt to novel situations. On the other hand, these skills do differ from one individual to another.

One of the basic misunderstandings that gets in the way of noticing how fundamental the creative process is for human beings is the assumption that we are not required to think creatively in our everyday world. The Greek philosopher Heraclitus told us long ago that we never step into the same river twice. Two experiences are never identical. If events are never the same, then we can never deal with life in the identical way we did before. Novelty and creativity are the norm, and we are always using the thought processes involved in producing new ideas and actions.

As Jean Piaget has taught us in our time, the first step in adaptation to life is to attempt to assimilate a new situation into our present knowledge. We attempt to match the new event with what we know. When the situation is so different that assimilation cannot be done, we need to change to meet the new situation. Our response accommodates to what is new. This is a process that goes on from the level of cells to the level of complex thinking. In fact, it is this adaptive ability that gives us our complex thinking, so elegantly imagined by Piaget as the development of cognitive structures. This is surprising only because we are unaccustomed to thinking about human adaptation, both assimilation and accommodation, as the imagination in action.

DISCUSSION

The creative process is fundamental to Godly play and to the theology of childhood. There is nothing new about this claim except, perhaps, a matter of emphasis or of detail. Placing this process at the center of our approach to religious education and in the center of our relationship to God has several interesting implications.

From the explorations of the imagination at the dawn of our civilization the conclusion emerged that the imagination involves a mixture of negation and freedom. It has elements of rebellion against the status quo and plunges us into change. Whether this is good or evil depends on the use to which the imagination is put. Whether to suppress or stimulate this unique human ability depends on whether it is used to create or to destroy life. To build we must often tear down to clear the way, so this is often very hard to determine.

The Incarnation focused the fullest expression of the ambiguity of the imagination. The story of one who was completely God and completely human made the intensity of this ambiguity available to us. Even as creatures of space and time we can enter deeply into the image and life of Christ. Our story can merge with God's story so that we could discover that we, too, are stretched on a cross, the cross of our human paradox. We are creatures of earth and sky, clay and spirit. We are an unstable mixture of the human and the divine. We need the stable paradox of Christ to stabilize our ambiguity and yet call us to use this unique quality to be creatures who are called upon to create rather than to destroy.

Philosophers have shown us that our calling involves us in both the reproduction of images stored in our memory and the production of new images. They have shown us that image production draws one into trusting the process, but that we also need to have the ability to use the imagination to keep our distance and be critical of what emerges. It is this double ability of entering and thinking about what is new that keeps us from becoming detached from reality, lost in the new as pure fantasy.

Other philosophers have shown us that there is a connection between the ability to make things strange and to make things familiar so we can live with them. The combination of the mysterious and the manageable seems to be something like a feedback loop, the one feeding into the other and itself being fed into, again and again, keeping life fresh.

The images that the imagination reproduces and produces point to different kinds of realities. The images of the artists, working in a variety of media, are the best examples of this. Some images point to God. Other images point to ourselves and the world. A third kind of images point to themselves. There are images that mirror eternity, images that mirror the earth and the self, and images that mirror the mirroring of images. Images can reflect God, the self and the world, and themselves. There is, perhaps, a fourth reality to be imaged that is as yet unknown. It is the mirror of the imagination itself. Perhaps that is what is being sought in the labyrinth of mirrors in postmodern art, but what if a better clue is the Holy Trinity, seen in a new way, without the three masks of Father, Son, and Holy Spirit? I shall return to this clue in the next chapter.

The levels of the imagination are not really distinct in the imagination's functioning. In reality the biological, the psychological, the social, and the spiritual aspects of the process are nested within each other and stimulate each other. It is only when they are separated for analysis that they can be spread out along a line of "levels." The imagination begins embedded in the biological. As we grow, it becomes psychological and social as it is differentiated to solve problems ranging from biological illness to existential aloneness, where our own participation in existence raises the spiritual issue.

One of the reasons that the social aspect of the levels must be included is that we learn so much about creativity from others. The so-called genius quality is in part socially defined and changes with time. Also, the creative process can be taught formally by showing how to remove blocks to the process. The assumption behind the creativity teaching movement is that creativity is not determined by stable traits like eye color. It works in all of us and at all levels.

The process of the imagination is at work in the amoeba adapting as well as in our own cells, and in our own intrapsychic, interpsychic, and spiritual dimensions. In the Christian tradition we use the interpretative frame of religious language formed by the canon of the Holy Scriptures, the liturgy of the church, and the parabolic aspect of both to come close to the Holy One.

Of course, our image of the imagination is anthropomorphic. It is what we do as human beings that interests us. We call "imagination" what we do when we put the imagination into action as the creative process. Amoebas and God know it as something else.

The fundamental ambiguity of the imagination is expressed most profoundly in its humble and yet grand use in the world of everyday. It does not need a special quality of leaps, genius, and unique forms of thinking to work. It works all the time, or we would be dead.

The pattern of the creative process is the stable point in change. Much as Wallas suggested in 1926, it moves from preparation to incubation to illumination to verification. In 1981 James Loder published *The Transforming Moment*[13] and made this pattern known to religious education and to pastoral counseling by involving the philosophy of Kierkegaard and his own counseling experience in its interpretation. The same process that is apparent in problem solving is also apparent in learning when we are the problem, as in an existential crisis.

There may be little need for an elaborate theory of the unconscious, as Weisberg has suggested, but it is important to have some way to account for the ability we have to sort through numerous aspects of a problem outside our consciousness. Michael

Polanyi spoke of focal and subsidiary interests. The inference is that we can't attend to everything at once, so some of the work must go on at some other "level" or in some other "place" outside our focal interest.

We are now at the very heart of the ambiguity of the imagination. Freud took us deeply into the ambiguity with a language of the unconscious, but it has been the split-brain research in modern times that has taken us more directly into the physiology of the matter. It is not surprising to me that one of the most intriguing and comprehensive of the books I have found during many years of reading in this area was written by James H. Austin, who has been involved in brain research for move than two decades. At the time he wrote his book *Chase, Chance and Creativity: The Lucky Art of Novelty,*[14] he was head of the department of neurology at the University of Colorado Medical School. This graduate of Brown University and Harvard Medical School is not only a researcher and physician but also a poet and the grand teller of a great tale.

Our left cerebral hemisphere thinks in verbal, auditory terms. It is good at translating symbols. It works best when analyzing a sequence of details. This is why it plays a dominant role when we talk, listen, or actively memorize. In contrast, our right hemisphere thinks in visual, nonverbal terms. It is good at complex spatial relationships. It specializes in three-dimensional depth perception. It also recognizes structural similarities and is best at drawing conclusions based on a grasp of a total visual picture, much as the Gestalt psychologists noticed. It is adept at incidental memorization and is the more musically gifted of the two hemispheres.

What does this have to do with the creative process and its ambiguity? The left hemisphere might put this question well and struggle to find the answer, but the right hemisphere "isn't talking." It is basically nonverbal. The source of intuitive insights is hidden away, almost out of the reach of language. The right hemisphere can't tell us in so many words what the sequences are that it experiences in this process. It is mute.

Austin pondered an additional feature about the brain and the creative process. The most remarkable thing is not that the two hemispheres are like an orchestra playing together. What is really interesting is that we also have at work "the conductor, one whose hand and baton will tell us whether the left, right, or both of our hemispheres are to be fully engaged."[15] It is enough trouble getting acquainted with the orchestra, but how will we meet the conductor? It is no wonder people over the ages have had such trouble explaining what happens in the moment of intuitive insight.[16] It is also why I refer to the moment of intuitive insight only as a "shifting of energy" without further elaboration.

This brings to a close our discussion of the imagination. We have taken a look at its complexity from several different angles.[17] In conclusion, however, we return to its fundamental ambiguity.

CONCLUSION

The ambiguity of the imagination is at the root of our being. To be alive we must create in biological, psychological, social, and spiritual ways. This is our destiny since Eden. It is a life guarded by an angel with a flaming sword where endings imply beginnings and beginnings imply endings. Life itself is a paradox that can be resolved only by the imagination in action, the creative process. This is how we are in the image of God.

7 The Theology of Childhood

Once, when I was about four or five years old, I was staying with my grandmother. At bedtime I crawled up into my grandfather's bed, since he was out of town, as were my parents. My grandmother had arthritis and walked with crutches, so when she got into bed she did so with difficulty, and then turned out the light. I remember the warm dark and the ticking of the clock, high up on the chest of drawers.

Despite the passing of almost five decades I still can feel vividly what happened next. The clean sheets sheltered me. The familiar smell of the room made me feel safe. I felt so good and alive that my skin tingled. My muscles moved for the sheer pleasure of feeling them respond. I stretched. Suddenly, as if a huge door opened in front of me, I sensed nothing—absolutely lightless nothing. "Grandmother! Why do I have to die?" I couldn't believe that the life I experienced so powerfully had to end.

My grandmother's words have vanished over time, but her presence in the dark and the sound of her voice are with me still. Somehow she put me in touch with a larger presence. I relaxed and slept soundly until morning, knowing my journey toward that presence had far to go.

I never told my parents about this episode, so my memory was not formed by their retelling of the story. The event has remained with me until now on its own, because of its significance. It continues to raise important questions for me. How did my grandmother help me with that fundamental question? What did she do? She had faced death herself with frankness, I am sure, so its reality did not frighten her into avoiding the question. She was deeply herself in her response. I remember nothing out of character, but how did that help? Why has this event had such a profound influence on my life? Where does the peacefulness it still gives me come from?

The theology of childhood is an attempt to answer such questions. This whole book comes from a growing awareness of how important and lasting the responses of adults are to such existential questions of children. It is also a call to hear such queries of children and to respect the experience they come from.

It is remarkable how many adults do respond with authentic honesty and wonder, like my grandmother, to the existential questions of their children, grandchildren, nephews, nieces, cousins, and young friends. These are moments that may never come again, so the children are fortunate to have such adults as part of their lives.

Godly play is an effort to give room and permission for existential questions to arise. It is a way to give children the means to know God better amid the community of children and with caring adults as guides. The theology of childhood is about a kind of knowledge. Godly play is about how to identify, name, and value it.

ANOTHER KIND OF KNOWLEDGE

Some people have concluded that children do not experience existential questions. This is more than an error in fact. Undervaluing the existential experience of children can be very destructive for their spiritual growth. The major refutation of such a conclusion is the large number of adults who, like myself, remember such experiences from their childhood. We do not usually talk about these events, so the oversight is understandable. These experiences do not get into the literature for the researchers to work with.

A major exception to the lack of reporting about children's religious experience in the research literature came from what is now called the Alister Hardy Research Center at Oxford. Sir Alister Hardy, a distinguished English biologist, founded the center in 1969. It was given his name after he died. Professor Hardy invited all those who "felt that their lives had in any way been affected by some power beyond themselves" to write an account of the experience and what it had meant to their lives. No mention was made of childhood. Edward Robinson, the second director, noticed that about 15 percent of the accounts received, some 600 of about 4,000 responses, referred to childhood experiences. His book *The Original Vision*[1] reported on and discussed the implications of these findings.

Robinson proposed that these reports of early religious experience suggested that there is a kind of knowledge that children have that goes undetected by cognitive developmental studies, such as those of Piaget. Piaget's starting point, and the starting point of many researchers, assumes that adult thinking is the norm, so the thinking of childhood is viewed as undeveloped adult thinking. If adult thinking is the measure of reality, then the child's view is a mistake. The inference is that education's task is to help nature liberate the child from this cognitive disability.

In the early 1960s Ronald Goldman wrote two important books that illustrate this viewpoint. He was struggling against the impression that the only difference between younger and older children in religious education was the amount of facts they ought to know. Verbal mistakes such as "Harold be thy name" in the Lord's Prayer concerned him. There was certainly more to religious education than quantity, he thought.

Goldman applied Piaget's research to religious knowing and concluded that young children got lost in the symbolic language of religion. It would be better, therefore, if the Bible, especially the parables, were reserved until adolescence, when symbolic language and analogy could be managed consciously and explicitly by what Piaget called "formal operations" logic.

With an unfortunate choice of words Goldman also concluded in his 1965 book *Readiness for Religion* that the period of early childhood was a "prereligious" period. He said, "In short, sin, death, frustration, enmity, lack of purpose, weakness, must have been known in some measure at first-hand if anyone is to feel the need to be saved from them. To put it another way, we need to have lived long enough to have experienced the real problems of the human condition before we see the point of what religion offers."[2] Certainly, children do not experience existential issues in the same way that adolescents and adults do, but that does not mean that they do not experience them in their own way.

In his 1964 book *Religious Thinking from Childhood to Adolescence* Goldman said, "Religious percepts and concepts are not based upon direct sensory data, but are formed from other perceptions and conceptions of experience. The mystics, who claim to have direct sensations of the divine, are exceptions, but as they are extremely rare cases, rarer in adolescence and practically unknown in childhood, we shall not explore their significance here."[3]

Goldman's books dominated about two decades of religious education, and much of his influence remains alive today. The claims that children do not experience existential issues and that children do not have religious experiences are both wrong. The weakening taboo against talking about mystical experiences is allowing a more balanced picture to emerge to counter this mistake.

Today there is a great deal of evidence in England and the United States that mystical experiences are more widespread than previously thought among adults. A later director of the Alister Hardy Center, David Hay, explored this matter and the causes for the taboo against talking about religious experience in his book *Exploring Inner Space: Is God Still Possible in the Twentieth Century?*[4] This religious form of knowledge among children deserves its own field of continued study, so well begun by Robinson.

Piaget, of course, never said that he was studying every kind of thinking used by children. He limited the scope of his inquiry to yield measurable results and to learn more about how one develops the skills needed for the scientific method. The questions that Piaget posed to young children were about the natural world, and they were the kinds of questions that could be answered by older children, using their greater verbal skills. This single line of research, however, left undetected the powerful nonverbal skills the young child uses to make meaning that were discussed in chapter 1 in connection with Winnicott's observations of mothers and babies.

What if the origins of the religious life and the special language for expressing and exploring the spiritual quest are to be found precisely there in silence? If that is true, a religious education limited to Piaget's vision of human thinking would be irrelevant to children and could even be damaging to their original form of knowing. It would teach by default that religious language is disconnected from their religious experience and the existential issues children intuit in their own way.

Part of the problem, it seems to me, is the definition of knowledge. Let us take the case of the conscious analogy, for example. Goldman, following Piaget, reasoned that since the conscious analogy is a mark of adolescent thinking, we may not expect children to think theologically by analogy before adolescence. He said that "religious insight generally begins to develop between twelve and thirteen years."[5] One of the kinds of thinking that goes undetected when we use such reasoning is what we might call a compressed, sensorial analogy used by younger children. Is it knowledge or not?

Such an intuitive relationship is certainly not one of the hallmarks of the scientific method. Teams of researchers, for example, could never use such personal intuitions in their joint work. Such sensorial logic, however, fits very well into the realm of theological cognition and even has a place in the creative aspect of scientific thinking. It is not included in finished scientific writing, but such poetry might aptly be used by those on a spiritual quest. Is the compressed, sensorial analogy a form of knowledge?

Did you ever watch ants as a young child? Robinson quoted at length from an ant story the writer remembered from fifty years before, when he was about five.[6] As the writer watched the ants, he knew that he was so big that the ants could not even know he was there. He was outside their knowledge, but as he turned away from his watching, he remembered, "I saw there was a tree not far away, and the sun was shining. There were clouds and blue sky that went on for ever and ever. And suddenly I was tiny—so little and weak and insignificant that it didn't really matter at all whether I existed or not."

He also wrote how a "watcher" would have had to be incredibly big to see him as he saw the ants in their world. Would the watcher be aware of him? Would he be aware of the watcher? He then wrote, "I *was* aware of him, in spite of my limitations. At the same time he was, and he was not, beyond my understanding." Not only was the young child making a compressed, sensorial analogy but he also was aware of the paradox in his thinking at some unspoken level that became explicit later, when he had the language ability to think and write about it. This sounds like knowledge to me. It is religious knowledge rather than scientific knowledge, that is all.

What happened next we adults need to pay particular attention to. The little boy went running into the house. Convinced that we are all part of the same sort of body, he announced happily, "We're like ants, running about on a giant's tummy!" No one understood what he was talking about, but, as he remembered it, that did not make any difference. "I knew what I knew," he wrote.

I, too, remember watching ants. In my case I was a year or two older, but I, too, look back over fifty years and clearly remember with my body what happened. It was summertime. I was killing ants by pounding them on the road with a hammer. They had made a den there that was breaking up the pavement. My father and I were going to destroy the den that evening, so I was taking matters into my own hands before he came home to take charge.

I still can feel my hand around the metal handle of the hammer and the sun on my back. Suddenly, without formulating any words, I stood up, turned around, and looked up into the heavens. The unspoken analogy was absolutely clear, words or not. How would I like it if God went around aimlessly pounding people in the way I was pounding ants? Others have told me of experiences with ants that evoked the same general and implicit analogy between people and ants. By the way, I asked my dad not to destroy the den, but he did anyway, since it was breaking up the road. It didn't matter. He was the one who did it, and I had tried to stop it. "I knew what I knew."

Piaget's research into how the child thinks about the natural world has been applied to the stages of the child's conception of death. But what is death? Is death like the mountain a child can drive around with his parents? Young children think there is a different mountain when they see it from a different angle and it has a different shape. Is thinking about death like thinking about whether the same amount of liquid in a tall, narrow container and in a low, wide one remains the same despite the two different shapes?

Death is not like a mountain, a liquid, or any other object in the natural world. How can Piaget's research be applied to the study of death? It is an absence rather than a presence. Furthermore, when it is one's own death that is involved, death becomes an existential mystery rather than a fact to be explained by the scientific method. Scientific language and religious language are very different in this regard. When someone dies, science wants to know the proximate cause. Religion invites people into the symbols and action of liturgical language, the funeral, to make religious meaning.

C. Daniel Batson and W. Larry Ventis concluded in their book *The Religious Experience: A Social-Psychological Perspective* that "to confront one's own death as an existential question, an individual must be able to imagine a time when he or she no longer exists, at least not in the ordinary sense of existence. The child does not ordinarily develop formal-operational thought of this kind until about ten years of age. Therefore, there is a long period when he or she lacks the mode of thought that would seem to be a prerequisite for understanding and appreciating the creative potential of religious symbols."[7]

Batson and Ventis published their excellent book in 1982. They even included an important discussion of what they call "the religious experience–creativity analogy" that is related to themes in this book. The quotation, however, points up the need not only for reported cases of children's expressions of existential questions and religious experience but also for a way to teach the creative potential of religious symbols to children. That is what Godly play is designed to do.

Adults can become too romantic about the supposed poetry and insight of young children. On the other hand, my experience with sick and dying children for more than a decade in the Texas Medical Center convinced me that young children know a lot about death and have religious experiences. I watched as children helped one another prepare for death when parents and other significant adults were not able to help them. I presented religious materials to them, especially the Parable of the Good Shepherd, and noticed a kind of peace visible in their faces and bodies even if they could not tell me why they felt peaceful. It was as if the little ones became wise beyond their size and years. At times the children even parented their parents as the end came near.

Medical play was developed to help the child cope with the fear of the unknown by learning about surgery and other procedures in the hospital with models and dolls. Such play also helps children express hurts and fears. What about the fear of death? Theological play with religious language was developed to help children cope with what cannot be known in the way things in the natural world can be known and that remains a mystery, even for adults.[8]

The religious life of the child is to be respected. A woman wrote in the Oxford study that the "most profound experience of my life came to me when I was very young—between four and five years old."[9] She identified the time by a favorite pair of shoes she was wearing. She and her mother were walking in "the moors" when the sun went down and a chill arose. She saw "a pearly mist" form. It swirled up around her ankles and hid her favorite black shoes with the silver buckles. Only the tallest harebells stood above this mystery.

She remembered understanding that the "shimmering gossamer tissue and the harebells," appearing here and there, were the "living tissue of life itself, in which that which we call consciousness was embedded, appearing here and there as a shining focus of energy in the more diffused whole. In that moment I knew that I had my own special place . . . and that we were all part of this universal tissue which was both fragile yet immensely strong, and utterly good and beneficent." It was many years later, while reading Traherne, Meister Eckhart, and Francis of Assisi, that the writer "cried aloud with surprise and joy, knowing myself to be in the company of others who had shared the same kind of experience and who had been able to set it down so marvellously."

It is important to present a few of these experiences to fill in the picture of the "original vision," as Robinson called it, but it is also important to expressly value such experience to overcome what is largely an adult oversight. One reason for the oversight is that it may take time to realize how important such original knowledge is. One writer wrote about the wholeness he experienced as a child and the openness with which he received life then. "I would compare that simple wholeness with the more complex wholeness that you work towards slowly. I think I am much more whole today at 81 than I was at 40."[10]

Sometimes children hang onto what they know by their original knowledge despite our best effort to make their knowledge conform to adult views. Sometimes a sense of the parent's or the church's God is formed that has little to do with the more powerful and present God that the child has experienced directly.

Somewhere between the ages of five and nine a little boy grew more and more outraged by the pictures at church that made Christ look like a weak person.[11] He also rejected the "miserable sinner" language of his Church of England worship experience. He wrote, "I hated it, and felt more and more strongly that it somehow blasphemed against the beauty, light and all-embracing fusion of God, man and matter which I thought I saw all around me."

When the boy was nine he "leapt up in the Church service, unable to bear the 'for there is no health in us' intoning any longer, and shouted that God wasn't like that at all; that he was nearer than one's own hand. And I was hustled out in floods of tears." He wrote that he was shaken by this event and begged not to be sent to church again. "My mother, while not comprehending my distress, allowed regular churchgoing to end at this point." Despite being silenced by misunderstanding and a lack of respect more surely and more deeply than adults have been silenced by official declarations of heresy, the child "knew what he knew."

THE SECOND GREAT GATE: LANGUAGE

The first great gate was discussed in chapter 1. It is there, through play, that we discover the exterior world, our own interior world, and the intermediate zone of play and transitional phenomenona between them. This is the reality gate. It is now time to discuss the second great gate through which all of us move into a second reality, the world of language, which has its own kind of reality.

Language gives us great power. It is not the villain of this story. Before language there is a tyranny of impulses, and waves of overpowering feelings rule us. Boundless fear and uncertainty roam there as well as wild ecstasy. Language gives us a way to stabilize things by gaining some distance from the direct coordination of actions. It gives us the perspective of time and space. The distance language gives us, then, is both the hero and the villain of the story.

Naming things is one of the helpful marks of growing up. It is also one of the marks of constructive therapy. You remember Rumpelstiltskin. He was the dwarf who helped the miller's daughter weave flax into gold. She was to give him her first-born child in return when she became queen. He appeared when the first child was born. The queen begged him to let her keep the child, but he would not give in. Finally, he told her that if she could discover his name by midnight of the third day she could keep the baby. When he appeared at midnight she was able to name him "Rumpelstiltskin," and he disappeared. Bringing conflicts and other problems into language can often reduce their power over us.

Look around. What do you see? Look carefully about the place in which you are reading. Can you see anything that does not have a name? Look carefully. Look between the things you can name. What is there? Is there any such "between"? Has language sealed us in?

Language creates the world we rely on as the fixed world. That is one of its virtues, but that is also one of its problems. Language can blind us to action itself. Take the coordination of action by which we curl up our hand into what we call a "fist." A "fist" is midway between the curling up and uncurling of the hand. Once we call that point in the coordination of actions a "fist," however, we don't see the whole process any longer.

Language also acts like a mirror to make us conscious of ourselves. Suppose there is a little girl named Alice. Her parents are going out. The baby-sitter comes, and Alice begins to fuss and carry on. She does not yet have language. She is swept by waves of powerful feelings and responds with tears and other expressions of her anxiety about the separation. One day, however, she says, "Alice cry." Suddenly, the child has entered language. She has seen herself in its mirror. The original coordination of actions is no longer primary. Her consciousness of that coordination of actions has now become primary.

Here is an illustration of what happens when the shift into language takes place among the fundamental relationships:

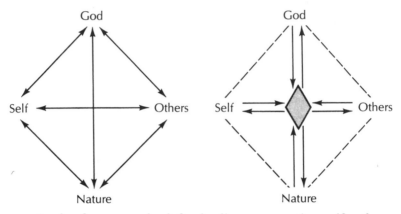

In the figure on the left, the lines connecting self, others, nature, and God are all solid, direct lines. Language is added to the illustration on the right. The primary relationships are now refracted through the prism of language. The primary relationships fade, as the dotted lines signify, in such a language world.

Language distances us from the direct experience of the primary relationships that make up our web of home. It can also block our perception of events when the prism of language acts like a mirror in front of our face so that we can see life only through a vision of ourselves seeing it. Words can stop the action of life, and our culture can turn what ought to be verbs into nouns when we learn language as children.

For example, rather than saying the name of God, "Yahwh," when it is written in the text, the Jewish tradition says "Lord." In this way the verb "Yahwh" (Exodus 3.14: "I Am Who I Am," or "I Am What I Am," or "I Will Be What I

Will Be") has had a better chance of remaining a verb, indicating the dynamic nature of God.

We human beings are happy to allow the coordination of actions by which we live to be turned into persons, places, or things and named as nouns, including God. If the world is full of nouns, then the world seems to be a more stable place. We feel more secure and we feel more in control.

During the development of language many special languages, such as those of science, ethics, art, and law, have originated to accomplish specific tasks. Schooling is usually required to acquire the vocabulary, logic, and tradition of such language domains. They do not exist independently of their use. We agree to speak and think in these special ways, and often we pay people—physicians, lawyers, ethics consultants, engineers, chemists, symphony conductors, and others—great sums of money to do so.

Science, for example, is a kind of language that generates sentences of explanation. It has a particular way to observe and define what it calls "facts," and it describes nature by means of these facts. Science explains nature by taking coordinations of action out of their ecology to name and control them in a particular way. The knowledge derived from such a controlled experiment is then reapplied to the world of everyday and assigned a certain probability for working out as predicted. If we were to speak of this view of the world as a language game we might call it the game of "Is" or "Probably Is."

The language world of ethics is very different. It is not a language of explanation and probability about the way nature works. It is a language that expresses values and organizes them in careful, logical ways—with special attention to the motive for the action, the action itself, and the results of the action—to decide what ought to be done in the natural world. If we were to think of ethics as a language game, we might call it the game of "Ought."

The language world of art is again different. It comprises neither explanations of nature nor recipes for good motives, action, or results. It is the expression in a variety of media about significance and beauty in the world. Some say it holds up a mirror to nature. Others say it is the unique expression of personal experience. Still others say that art is the coordination of surface relationships on the work of art itself so that it refers only to itself. Whatever the view of what is happening in art, there is an agreement that art is not the real world. The language game of art might be called the game of "Pretend."

The Anglo-Saxon tradition of law is a language created by the decisions of judges about particular cases. These cases provide a history and a kind of logic to use with facts decided by juries and with laws passed by legislatures so that decisions can be reached that in turn will influence future cases. These decisions are enforced by the power of the state. Force is what makes this language game the game of "Must." It is not about recommending or suggesting.

We get into trouble with language domains when we try to use the wrong tool for the task we want to accomplish. Using the wrong language tool is like trying to play tennis with a football. We can also get caught in cross-gaming in similar games. The tennis ball from the next court might bounce into our court of play so we don't know which one to hit back. This means that teachers who invite children into a particular kind of language need to be very careful. To teach children to use one kind of language, such as religious language, in the way that another kind of language—such as science, ethics, art, or law—is used could be to teach its misuse.

How are we using language at this moment? It is not like the language of science, ethics, art, or law. It is not religion. This is philosophy. We are using language to discuss language itself. Such a task can make one dizzy, but it is the only way we have to understand language or to design experiments to add to our empirical knowledge of it.

What, then, is religious language? Religious language helps us come closer to God and the whole network of self, others, nature, and God. This is a language of mystery. It asks us to discover a presence at the edge of our being and knowing, but it is not a presence we can look at directly. That would be like moving directly toward the horizon. As we advance, the horizon retreats. What religious language invites us to do is to enter into its actions, symbols, narratives, and parables to play at the edge of our existence. It is then that the presence of God may come to be with us. Religious language, then, is a language of excla-

mation. If we were to give this language game a name, we
might call it "Wow!"

Religious language is the way we make meaning at the limits of being and knowing. It puts the other kinds of language
into perspective. It says that the experience of facts, values,
beauty, and justice are all important, but not one of these
standpoints in the world is the ultimate one. The ultimate
standpoint is at the edge of our existence, where we sense the
presence of God.

This is not to say that the domain of religious language is
relegated to the edge of the world of everyday. Death, the
threat of freedom, the need for meaning, and our aloneness all
break through into the center of that world. This is true despite our best efforts to build up walls of language to keep such
issues at bay so we can presume to take control of life.

The edge or limit is a line marked by paradoxes we can
neither break through nor escape. They permeate our everyday world. We are born, yet we die. Why? We need company,
but we are existentially alone, having to be born and to die for
ourselves. Why? We cry out for freedom but usually only from
positions of slavery, because we are fearful of freedom. Why?
We need meaning, but the meaning we know we need we often
want to hide from. Why? These paradoxes box us in and bind
us, but they also define who we are as human beings.

There is nothing especially new about what I am saying. It
has been said often in various ways through the centuries.
What is important here is how this affects the teaching of the
art of using religious language today. Our modern world of
electronic communications has blurred the edges of language
domains. Religious language has become tangled up with fund
raising, the casual phrases of the civil religion, the wide variety
of religious traditions, and even the advertising of automobiles.
What does religious language do best?

TEACHING THE UNIQUENESS OF
RELIGIOUS LANGUAGE

Sensing the existential limit of our being and knowing causes
us to draw in our breath. There is inspiration. When breath is

released, exclamations shade into one another with overlapping meanings. First, a sound like "AHH!" can be heard. This sigh suggests the presence of the nourishing mystery that feeds and yet overwhelms us with awe.

The awe shades into another experience that involves more awareness of what is going on. We might say, "AHA!" The expelling of air now has an inflection in it. This exclamation indicates that we have identified the experience. The ecstasy of the sigh shades into the exclamation of discovery. For discovery to take place, a split must open up between the "I" and the "Other."

The third step in this awareness is to sense the paradoxes about knowing God. We realize that to be aware of knowing God means that we have already stepped out of the primary experience itself. In addition to the primary split between the self and God another one is also sensed, the split between the "I" and the "me" who are thinking together about this. These discoveries erupt into "HAHA!"—the sometimes smaller and sometimes greater bursts of air we call laughter. Sometimes we even laugh until we cry or cry until we laugh. This is the third paradox, the one where laughter and tragedy stimulate each other.

These experiences can be shown in a kind of feedback loop. The primary experience shades into an awareness of the experience and then into the awareness of the paradox that binds our experience of God. To know is not to know the Holy One.

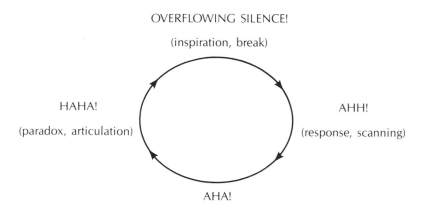

OVERFLOWING SILENCE!

(inspiration, break)

HAHA!   AHH!

(paradox, articulation)   (response, scanning)

AHA!

(awareness, insight)

The experience of God might be a gradual or a dramatic and sudden event. However it takes place, our circle of meaning is opened or broken, so we begin to scan to put it back together again. From the scanning comes the birth of a new way to see the world. It is then that we realize that we no longer know directly what first prompted us to change. Let us now add to the complexity of this simple loop of original knowledge by showing how religious language is rooted in it.

The "AHH!" is related to the encounter with God and the sigh of ecstasy. This unitive experience helps us discover the deep integration of the self that takes into consideration our existential limits as well as the nourishment of being in touch with God. This is too much meaning for language to bear, which explains why what we do and show in liturgy is so important. This is why the integration this encounter can foster is so deep.

The "AHA!" of discovery introduces the possibility of reflection on the experience of God by putting some distance between us and the primary experience. We are no longer so much in the experience that we are overwhelmed. We are beginning to notice it. This notice takes the form of narrative.

The master story for Christians is a journey with the "elusive presence"[12] of God. We move closer to and then more distant from the Holy One as we proceed. Our story's fundamental meaning is discovered in the master story. This aspect of the experience brings with it a sense of identity for this reason.

The "HAHA!" exclamation marks the awareness of the paradox that stimulates the imagination to recover what is no longer present to it in experience. Paradoxical language also prevents the reduction of the mystery of God's presence into ordinary language. Paradox is the soil from which parables grow.

When the experience breaks into language, there is another layer of experience, but this time it is involved with the structures and reflection of language. In a second level of experience the sigh of awareness is shaped by the symbols and action of liturgy. The awareness of insight becomes the narrative line of the sacred story. The paradox takes the form of parables.

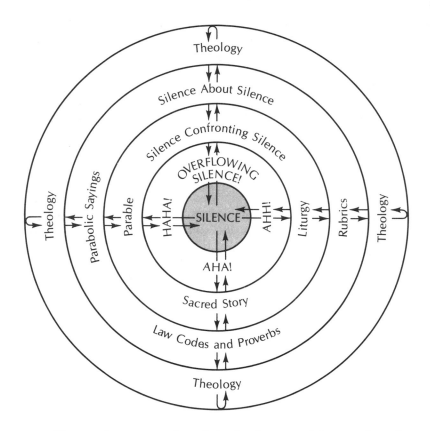

To use the geography of the brain, we might say that the encounter of God is a right-brained kind of knowledge that gives us integration. It orients us in a larger kind of space and time. When the experience of God shifts to the form of story, it enters space and time. The journey with the elusive presence of God refers one outside space and time, but consciousness is limited to the edge of our own being and knowing. It moves from a beginning through a middle to an end. Parables use language to force us back into the domain of the right brain, the place for orienting ourselves in the larger space and time beyond language.

More layers of language can be laid over the original ones. The inner core of the experience is silence. The first layer, already mentioned, is not yet in language but is a primary kind of integration, identification, and arousal of the imagination marked by exclamation. The second layer is in language. It is the kind of language that deeply involves one in the experience itself. This is the layer of liturgy, sacred story, and parable.

The third layer of experience is another step toward abstraction. Instead of the action and symbol of liturgy itself there are the rubrics, the language about how to perform liturgy. Instead of sacred story there are the summaries of the master story in law codes and proverbs. Instead of the parables themselves there are parabolic sayings and aphorisms.

The outer layer of these circles of meaning is the domain of theology. Theology is language about God. We have moved from being speechless to being in language, to using language to speak about God.

The task of theology is to be sure that our use of this powerful language is balanced. This means that a theologian needs to be much more than a historian or a systematic logician. If the fundamental experience is not present to this person, then the reference point for the whole language system cannot be understood. Without the original vision theology becomes mere words about words.

Of course, language shapes our experience, and our experience shapes our language. This is a matter of developmental timing rather than a logical issue. What is important to notice about the original vision and cognitive development is that primary knowledge might break through at any time in one's life. The theology of childhood is not just about children. It is about the experience of God and what develops from that.

One can move back and forth among these layers of experience and meaning. There are developmental implications, however. Young children are the most limited. Adults sometimes choose to return to earlier levels of language and experience, but children have no choice but to remain where they are. Only maturation allows them to perform the more abstract and complex operations that are required at the later (or outer) levels suggested above.

You may have experienced what happens when religious language gets out of balance. Liturgy turns into ritualism, a meaningless repetition of actions. When the sacred story dominates, scripture becomes worshiped in itself as if it were God. Parable turns sour and degenerates into sarcasm when it dominates. The balanced interaction among these three functions and silence prevents a winding down of their collective creative power. That winding down turns religious language into a still powerful but destructive version of its intended use.

Godly play identifies, names, and values the religious language domain, and its deep wellspring of silence. It does the same for the subfunctions—liturgy, sacred story, and parable. Children need to sense this organization and balance from an early age as part of the art of the language's use. This is not to say that children can talk about this. It is largely their senses that inform them of the structure and function of the language system. How this happens was covered in chapter 5.

What is needed today more than ever is a strong sense of what one's tradition is. It is difficult to have an appreciation for the complexity of someone else's tradition if one's own is unknown. How can we even know what religion is, when its language blends together with other domains that have nothing to do with existential issues or religious experience? Such pressures and questions call attention to the need to give children a deep but open and flexible grounding in their own traditions.

THE MIND OF THE MAKER

Dorothy Sayers was born in 1893 in the shadow of Tom Tower and within the sound of its bell in Oxford. Her father was headmaster of the Choir School at Christ Church College. Dorothy's nurse later told her that she had been noticed by the shy, retired professor of mathematics and logic who wrote *Alice in Wonderland* under the pen name Lewis Carroll. The elderly don with the mane of wavy gray hair would meet them walking and stop to smile at her in her baby buggy.

Many others were to notice Dorothy. T. S. Eliot, C. S. Lewis, Charles Williams, J.R.R. Tolkien, and other literary giants found that she could clearly hold her own among them. Dorothy took First Class Honors in Medieval Literature at Oxford in 1915. She went from there to London, where she worked for nearly a decade in an advertising agency. Dorothy was clearly a pioneering and talented young woman.

The detective stories Dorothy wrote, centering on Lord Peter Wimsey, began to be a great success during her lifetime and continue to be read today and enjoyed in their television versions as well. She was a poet, a playwright, a lay theologian, a scholar of medieval texts and languages, a church warden at St. Thomas's Church on Regent's Street in London, and an advocate of the Christian Way, which she saw as being not only true but an adventure, intellectually respectable and fun.

In 1941, when she was close to fifty, Dorothy wrote *The Mind of the Maker*.[13] In this book she rejected the view that life's meaning could be reduced to a series of solvable problems she called "detective problems." She asserted that the only way to understand life was to understand the creative mind of the creature and by analogy the mind of God, the Creator.

A detective problem is always solvable. In fact, it is constructed for the express purpose of being solved. Further, a detective problem is *completely* solvable. There are no loose ends or "unsatisfactory enigmas" left anywhere. A third characteristic of detective problems is that they are solved in the same terms in which the problem is set. Finally, the detective problem is finite. When it is solved, that is the end of it.

The fallacy of looking at life as a problem is that such a view excludes from life everything that such tidy solutions cannot solve. For example, the human search for peace cannot be contained in closed solutions. To think of the search as a problem that can be solved, of peace as something attainable once and for all, is to reduce a dynamic process to "detective problem" status. Solutions do not last when people are involved. Only a continuing labor of creation endures.

If human issues cannot be reduced to problems, how are we to find our way? What are we to teach children, if not how to solve problems and get answers? If all is process, what is the pattern of the process? How can this be taught?

To answer such questions, Sayers spoke of her personal experience of the creative mind. She argued that this pattern "corresponds to the actual structure of the living universe" so that when people feel powerless in this universe it means that they are at odds with it. Their lives and work have become distorted and run counter to the universal pattern.

She wrote: "If you ask me what is this pattern that I recognize as the true law of my nature, I can suggest only that it is the pattern of the creative mind—an eternal idea, manifested in material form by an unresting energy, with an outpouring of power that at once inspires, judges, and communicates the work; all these three being one and the same in the mind and one and the same in the work. And this, I observe, is the pattern laid down by the theologians as the pattern of the being of God."[14]

This pattern is as real as gravity, which operates alike on apples and solar systems. The creative process is present alike in the Creator and in every creature. This does not mean that everyone is supposed to go off and write poetry or music. Such a thought only shows how wide the gaps have become between art, life, and science. What we are all called to do is to become artists in living. The material with which we all create is life itself.

This means that we need to treat life as all creators treat their materials. The goal of life is not to overcome it, as the mistaken metaphor of the king or rescuing savior might suggest. Such views of life give up our freedom to create and to help one another create. The goal is to cooperate with life in love.

We need to be well aware that the way of creation settles nothing once and for all. That is not the goal. As Sayers said, "The thing that is settled is finished and dead." The person who looks at life as if it were a problem to be solved, once and for all, is concerned with death and not with life. The person who looks at life like an artist sees it as the medium for creation. The seeker finds the treasure to be in the seeking. As we shall see in a moment, Gregory of Nyssa used the metaphor of Moses to say much the same thing in the fourth century after Christ.

The ideas of Dorothy Sayers are important for the theology of childhood and Godly play because the "subject matter" to be taught is God. This is not like teaching how to solve detective problems. God, after all, is limited only by the fact that God is not limited. This was the primary theme of Gregory of

Nyssa's meditation *The Life of Moses*,[15] written about A.D. 390, when he was around sixty years old.

A young monk, Caesarius, had asked Gregory for advice to guide his journey toward God through the discovery of a life of perfect virtue. Gregory began by saying that God provided examples for men and women to follow in the lives of Abraham and Sarah. The migration of Abraham and Sarah was no mere geographical journey; nor were the journeys of Moses. Both were a stretching of the human consciousness and capacity to know God. Gregory decided to use the story of Moses to guide Caesarius and so guides us with it as well. Moses followed God all his life, but he never found the Holy One still. God was always moving on ahead of Moses, even on Mt. Sinai.

Knowing God, Gregory said, is not something one can accomplish in a once-and-for-all way. He used Paul's metaphor from his letter to the Phillippians about running a race to clarify this idea. There is no stopping place, no finish line, in time and space for this race. One does not become fed up with the desire for the spiritual quest, as one does for ordinary running, because God continues to call us forward.

Paul said, "I press on toward the goal for the prize of the upward call of God in Christ Jesus. Let those of us who are mature be thus minded; and if in anything you are otherwise minded, God will reveal that also to you" (3.13–16).

There are two kinds of spiritualities. One is dynamic and eternally on the move, like that of Gregory. The other attempts to achieve a kind of wholeness one can hang on to. Gregory's dynamic and moving spirituality has a focus on the "upward call," the blessing and creating aspect of creation. Achievement spirituality has a focus on the threat of sin and the need for salvation. The first is based on the love of creating. The second is based on the fear of falling. Both are realistic. They are joined into one spirituality when we realize that it is only by creation that we can overcome destruction.

But how can we teach this to children? We teach religious language as framed by the canon of the Bible, or "God's autobiography," as Dorothy Sayers called it. When the subject of the story is God, the Being who is limited only by being unlimited, the nature of the autobiography becomes very interesting.

When an idea becomes a book, the book actualizes the power of the idea, but it also limits it. An autobiography is only one of a writer's created works, yet it is an interpretation of the whole series. A great deal of the power of the author's personality can be sensed in such a work. Even an autobiography, however, cannot contain the whole author. This is even truer of God.

How, then, can we know the author from the book? As Sayers put it: "By our response to it, we are brought within the mind of the author and are caught up into the stream of his Power, which proceeds from his Energy, revealing his Idea to us and to himself."[16] It is this "response" that we can teach by showing children how we respond to God's autobiography—the sacred story, the parables, and the liturgy that flow out and point back to the unspoken energy of the creator.

Godly play and the theology of childhood are especially relevant for our time because many adults are now discovering that they are grounded in a false self. They sense that there is another and truer self they have covered over by always being what others wanted them to be. The inner child awaiting discovery is full of energy, creative, spontaneous, and deeply centered. The theology of childhood is about children and adults discovering that child. Godly play is a way to keep open the opportunity for the true self to emerge in childhood and the possibility that adults may return to where they began and begin to grow again.

Notes

CHAPTER 1. Playing and Reality

1. Clark C. Abt, *Serious Games* (New York: Viking Press, 1970).
2. Abt, *Serious Games*, p. 6.
3. Robert S. De Ropp, *The Master Game* (New York: Dell Publishing, A Delta Book, 1968), p. 13.
4. Roland H. Bainton, *Here I Stand: A Life of Martin Luther* (Nashville: Abingdon Press, 1950), p. 42. The following quotations from Bainton are from pp. 45, 51, and 54.
5. Adam Phillips, *Winnicott* (London: Fontana Press, 1988), p. 34.
6. D. W. Winnicott, *Playing and Reality* (London: Tavistock Publications, 1971).
7. Catherine Garvey, *Play* (Cambridge, MA: Harvard Univ. Press, 1977). Garvey's book is not, of course, the only or even the primary classic about play. A clear and succinct survey of the field may be found in Brian Sutton-Smith's chapter "Children's Play: Some Sources of Play Theorizing" in *Children's Play*, No. 9, New Directions for Child Development, Kenneth H. Rubin, guest ed. (San Francisco: Jossey-Bass Publishers, 1980).
8. Hugo Rahner, S. J., *Man at Play* (London: Burns and Oates, 1965), pp. 19–25.
9. Umberto Eco, *The Name of the Rose* (New York: Harcourt Brace Jovanovich, 1983). The original Italian was published by Gruppo Editoriale Fabbri-Bompiani, Sonzogno, Etas S.p.A. A very useful interpretation that includes both questions of history and the modern theory of signs is Theresa Coletti, *Naming the Rose: Eco, Medieval Signs, and Modern Theory* (Ithaca and London: Cornell Univ. Press, 1988).
10. Eco, *The Name of the Rose*, p. 585.
11. Walter Lowrie, *A Short Life of Kierkegaard* (Princeton: Princeton Univ. Press, 1942), p. 14.

12. Søren Kierkegaard, *Purity of Heart Is to Will One Thing* (New York: Harper and Row, Torchbook Edition, 1956), p. 181.
13. Karl Jaspers, *The Great Philosophers* (New York: Harcourt, Brace and World, Helen and Kurt Wolff Book, 1966), p. 210. I first noticed something like this "ball game" of Cusanus in Hermann Hesse's novel *Magister Ludi*. It came to light again in an important background book for Godly play, David Miller's *Gods and Games* (New York: Harper and Row, Colophon Books, 1973). Reference to Cusanus's game is found there on pages 163–164.

A lovely introduction to Nicholas of Cusa is Jasper Hopkins's *Concise Introduction to the Philosophy of Nicholas of Cusa* (Minneapolis: Univ. of Minnesota Press, 1978).
14. Sofia Cavalletti, *The Religious Potential of the Child* (New York/Ramsey: Paulist Press, 1983). I first saw Dr. Cavalletti present this material to a child during the winter of 1970–1971 in Bergamo, Italy. I have worked with this approach to religious education ever since.

I began to think of this approach to religious education as a kind of "worship-education" during the summer of 1982 while I was working on the preface to the English edition for Cavalletti's book *The Religious Potential of the Child*, which I arranged to have published in English. I began the preface by referring to Cavalletti's "worship-education center in Rome" (p. 3).

CHAPTER 2. An Adult at Play

1. George Miller, "The Magical Number Seven Plus-or-Minus Two: Some Limits on Our Capacity for Processing Information," *Psychological Review* 63 (1956): 81–97.
2. James E. Loder, Mary D. Synnott Professor of the Philosophy of Christian Education, Theological Seminary, Princeton, NJ.

CHAPTER 3. Children at Play

1. Howard Gardner, *Frames of Mind: The Theory of Multiple Intelligences* (New York: Basic Books, 1983).
2. Maria Montessori, *The Child in the Church* (St. Paul, MN: Catechetical Guild, 1965). This book collects the writings of and about Montessori and religious education. Further orientation can be found in Jerome W. Berryman, "Montessori and Religious Education," *Religious Education* 75 (May–June 1980). In addition, please see chapter 5.
3. If Jesus had wished to compare smallness and largeness or power and weakness by using a "tree" and its small seed, he could have used the more traditional symbol of power and royalty, the cedars of Lebanon. The parable must, therefore, carry more meaning than this simple comparison.

The Greek uses "shrub" rather than "tree." On the other hand, "tree" communicates better to young children. The "tree" in the material is about the same relative size to the figure planting the seed as a mustard shrub in Israel today is to a six-foot-tall person. A photograph is even included in the parable box of such a person beside the mustard shrub. This leaves the way open to work with the older children about why Jesus didn't say "tree."

4. James E. Loder, *The Transforming Moment: Understanding Convictional Experiences* (San Francisco: Harper and Row, 1981).
5. Irvin D. Yalom, *Existential Psychotherapy* (New York: Basic Books, 1980). This book provides a useful synthesis of psychology and existential philosophy in reference to life's limits.

CHAPTER 4. The Spoken Lesson

1. Eric Havelock, *Preface to Plato* (Cambridge, MA: Belknap, 1963).
2. Werner Kelber, *The Oral and the Written Gospel* (Philadelphia: Fortress Press, 1983).
3. Kelber, *The Oral and the Written Gospel*, p. 158.
4. David H. Kelsey, *The Uses of Scripture in Recent Theology* (Philadelphia: Fortress Press, 1975), pp. 89–119; see especially p. 106.
5. Gregor T. Goethals, *The TV Ritual: Worship at the Video Altar* (Boston: Beacon Press, 1981), p. 143.
6. Thomas E. Boomershine, "Locating the Electronic Church in the History of Religious Communication," paper presented for the Children, Religion and Television Symposium, Institute of Religion, Texas Medical Center, Houston, 1983. This seminar, hosted by Jerome Berryman, also included presentations by the host ("The Hermeneutics of Television"), by Hedda Bluestone Sharapan of "Mr. Rogers Neighborhood" ("Conceptualizing a Children's Television Show"), and by William Martin of Rice University ("The Electronic Preacher").
7. Jean Leclercq, O.S.B., *The Love of Learning and the Desire for God: A Study of Monastic Culture*, 3d ed. (New York: Fordham Univ. Press, 1982). See especially pp. 72–77.
8. Harvey Cox, *The Seduction of the Spirit: The Use and Misuse of People's Religion* (New York: Simon and Schuster, 1973).

CHAPTER 5. The Unspoken Lesson

1. Urban T. Holmes, *Ministry and Imagination* (New York: Seabury Press, 1976), pp. 134–136.
2. Bruce Reed, *The Dynamics of Religion: Process and Movement in Christian Churches* (London: Darton, Longman & Todd, 1978).
3. The first model presented below for comparison is based on personality types. The second model is based on a center of balance

among historical examples of destructive movements. My approach is to divide people into thinking and feeling types, as the other two examples have done, but to combine that spectrum of knowing preference with one involving tendencies toward closure and openness. This is because these two pairs of opposites fit better with the creative process and because of their relevance to both worship and religious education practice.

Michael and Norrisey named their spirituality types after four well-known saints: St. Ignatius of Loyola, St. Francis of Assisi, St. Thomas Aquinas, and St. Augustine of Hippo. The difference among these four people becomes immediately apparent and provides us with a map to distinguish spiritual differences. Their typology is based on the Myers-Briggs Type Indicator and its revision by David Kiersey. Chester P. Michael and Marie C. Norrisey published this model in their book *Prayer and Temperament: Different Prayer Forms for Different Personality Types* (Charlottesville, VA: The Open Door, 1984).

Urban T. Holmes presented a typology related to the history of Christian spirituality in *A History of Christian Spirituality: An Analytical Introduction* (New York: Seabury Press, 1980). He associated thinking with an active approach and opposed it to feeling, which he associated with passivity. The other axis of the grid opposed the approaches to knowing God by emptying oneself of images and at the other extreme by the visualization of images. In the center there is a circle of balanced wholeness.

When the four tendencies are balanced, one's spirituality is considered to be whole and creative. When combinations of the dimensions, such as a pull toward emptying and thinking, pull away from the center of balanced wholeness and get stuck there, a pathology develops. The pathologies were defined in historical terms by this model.

Active thinking and imaging produce a distortion toward rationalism. Imaging and passive feeling combine to produce the distortion of pietism in the sense of sentimental Biblicism that is anti-intellectual and flourishes in self-congratulatory small groups.

When active thinking and emptying are associated, one gets a distortion toward asceticism that is anti-worldly and anti-physical. When emptying oneself of images and passive feeling are associated, there is a tendency toward the distortion of quietism, a reduction toward passive reception. It is indicated by becoming stuck in surrender, intuition, surprise, and anti-structure.

4. Søren Kierkegaard, *Concluding Unscientific Postscript* (Princeton: Princeton Univ. Press, 1941), p. 311.

5. James W. Fowler, *Stages of Faith: The Psychology of Human Development and the Quest for Meaning* (San Francisco: Harper and Row, 1981). I first became interested in Fowler's work in the early

1970s. A conference at the Institute of Religion resulted in a book, which I edited: *Life Maps: Conversations on the Journey of Faith* (Waco, TX: Word Press, 1978). A second edition was published in 1985 with a new concluding chapter by this author discussing the two points of view that James Fowler and Sam Keen presented in the book.

Fowler's data have shown that after children leave behind a period of relative linguistic silence about the age of two years, they enter a time that develops into the use of episodic language to put their world together. The world is structured like a handful of pearls. It rolls around in pieces. It won't stay put. It is not coherent by itself without being grasped by the hand, or being held together by the presence of primary adults. A stable world cannot yet be "grasped" by the mind.

By about seven years of age, the child—now in grammar school—is able to string together the handful of pearls. This is the time of story—beginning, middle, and end. World coherence is founded on tales of significant people and action. The pearls can be strung together on a string of narrative.

By adolescence, sometimes as early as twelve years of age, there is a tendency to put the stories of significance together into a master story. It may be in terms of family, the teenager's personal story, the story of a hero, the story of scripture, or some other story. This is a story about all other stories that gives them a coherence beyond the stringing together of episodes. Each narrative strand of pearls is now part of a larger story.

Sometimes as early as age twenty some people develop an ability to use language in a way that rejects narrative as the most important form of conceptualization. Narrative is replaced by abstractions. The adolescent often can think about his or her own thinking and form hypothetical cases about the world, but that approach to life is not fully worked out. Often it still needs the support of teachers, workbooks, and other explicit, step-by-step guides. During their twenties many people begin to do this in a more comprehensive and self-directed way.

Notice that the development from the episodic use of language to narrative to the master story to abstractions gives the growing person more and more control over the way the coordination of actions in the world is given coherence. After a person lives for a while in a conceptual world tied together by formal logic, a sense of apparent control begins to take over the coordination of actions in which one is embedded. This can be shattered by a break in one's health, the loss of a loved one, or some other crisis over which one has no control.

The fifth layer of language works something like this. When you or I are before the elements of Holy Communion, we might make an analysis using the logic, concepts, and grammar of the domains of psychology, sociology, physics, biology, or any other language tools we have learned to use in our schooling. What is discovered in this stage is that one cannot participate in Holy Communion while studying it. One needs to set aside the abilities built up over many decades to participate, as one did as a child, to find the kind of truth that is awaiting us in that language domain that is appropriate for the existential issues of religion.

The sixth and last layer of language is one that is silent, somewhat like the "language" of pre-language children. Because of this silence, investigation is difficult by the interview approach. While the infant's silence was naive, this silence is not. It is wise and profound. The value of being with God far exceeds the value of talking about God.

In Fowler's analysis the beginning and ending stages are very important clues for understanding the function of religious language. At the other stages it is assumed that one can construe and control the world by a developing logical structure. All that differs is the kind of structure. It is quite clear, however, that before language and at the "end" of language such control is impossible or realized to be impossible. One is too aware of the actual coordination of actions. It is not until stage six that the Fowler people really begin to ask why they should continue to try to control the world rather than letting go and letting be. The answer is that there is no answer. There is relationship with a presence unlike what is present in the natural world, and this experience of presence cannot be reduced to words.

The language of reflection has a wide use in the church, but the language of mystery is what the church can contribute that science, law, ethics, and other language domains do not, powerful and important as they may be. In *The Language of Mystery* (London: SCM Press, 1987), Edward Robinson speaks of the vertical and the horizontal mystery. The first is for going beyond the limits of what is known. The second is for communicating that experience to others.

Robinson argued that the language of mystery is rooted in the reality of the Mystery rather than being an escape into fantasy. It needs both tradition and the creative impulse toward the new to be healthy. Above all, participation in the language of mystery is not something someone can do for you. Authority for the use of this language comes from having encountered the Mystery and having come back. Such people do not explain this; they only show that the journey is possible and that it is required of all.

Attention is paid to nonverbal communication in this approach to religious education, because the coordination of action it reflects is profoundly important to human identity and growth. The language of mystery is to be played with for itself. It can lead us back into direct experience of the pure coordination of actions with the Holy. It is the way out of being the observer that language turns us into by its mirror and a way into the being it takes to know Being. Such identity is renewing and renews others.

6. Consider the symbol of the cross. Put yourself in front of the image. You move your eyes over it and then begin to focus on it. Your eyes begin to lose their focus. The cross blurs. It disappears. As this is happening, you begin to move into the cross's meaning—the story from Nativity to Easter to Pentecost to now. Faces merge and overlay the cross. Faces of mystery and faces you sometimes recognize part of. You lose track of time. . . .

The cross again is there. You notice what is behind the cross and run your eyes over its details. You might remember where your father used to sit in church and the stained glass window to the right of the pew. Your mother always sat to your left. A kind of daydreaming continues, and then you are finished.

You cross yourself (if that is your custom) and stand (if your custom is to kneel), and you take your leave. As you walk away from the cross, you feel strangely refreshed. New images begin to enter your mind about unrelated things. The day goes on. The unrelated images become ideas. Meaning and direction have been reshaped.

This process begins with a kind of active openness. The openness is wonder, opening the door of the language of Mystery so that it can do its work. It is opening the creative process to the Creator. It is waiting for the birthing process. It is a playfulness, a willingness to play with the Holy. It is Godly play. Nothing special happened, and yet it did. It is very hard to know what, since the act of origination applied to one's own existential meaning is not yet "in language" so that we might study it.

Certainly, there is more here than meets the eye. I have tried to describe in narrative how it might be during a fairly uneventful entering into a liturgical symbol. Now I would like to talk *about* the cross to suggest the difference between being in its symbol and talking about it.

The intersection of the cross is absorbed by babies while peering into the crossing of the line of the eyes and the line made by the nose and the mouth in the face of the mother and the father leaning over the crib. The child absorbs that image before language and associates it with the sensations surrounding that period of life. This is not to say that the final meaning and emotional connotation of the cross can be reduced to this primary experience, but it is to say that the cross is a fundamental image of life, like bread, water, and wine.

Later another intersection of lines might be pointed to by a parent in church or some other place. Perhaps the sign of the cross is made over oneself or with the thumb on the forehead of the child. The symbol is identified, named, and valued. It is a "cross." The coordination of action with the intersection of lines is named and fixed, but for the child it is not yet part of the larger system of symbols we call "Christian."

A third step occurs when this "piece" of language is associated with the religion one belongs to. One belongs to something marked with the cross. The question "What is a Presbyterian or Roman Catholic?" is usually answered at this stage by talking about the building where one goes to church, but by this time the cross may signal a part of the story of Christ. It may also signal a blessing.

During elementary school a variety of cross images are experienced. They give added dimensions to the symbol. Variety is also noted in the contextual meaning of the crossed lines. Roads cross. When working with numbers a cross is a "plus sign" and means addition. Strange, bent variations of the cross can mean "Hitler." Turning the symbol half on its side means "multiplication." The cross as a symbol is becoming more complex, and at the same time the cross of Christianity is becoming more and more specific as a symbol. The cross may now also symbolize the whole story of Christ.

Talk about crosses and the Christian cross again begins to shift during middle school and high school. Awareness of different religions becomes more explicit, and their primary symbols can be compared to the cross. Such distinctions can begin to make the cross even more a sign of one's identity, but in a more formal way than before. It can also be a symbol that one resists or rebels against. The cross symbolizes the church and what it stands for. It may mean authority, irrelevant words and actions, and other things that are positive or negative or a mixture of both.

The years of college and young adulthood pass. The valuing of persons and places where one first experienced the cross sinks into a kind of tacit knowing. From time to time one might acknowledge the cross, as in a procession or on another formal occasion, but little is done to bring out what the cross means now at this adult stage. If there is a tragedy one might become involved with the cross in a deeper way, but usually things go on with a lighter step. Children begin to arrive. Finally, one begins to wonder how to connect the religion of childhood and adolescence with where one is now in life. Ultimate questions about the cross and its meaning begin to work their way back into life.

During the period of young adulthood one may begin to use some of the tools learned in college and elsewhere to analyze religion. Philosophy of language, anthropology, psychology, sociology, and all the other "-ologies" can be applied to understanding the cross. This keeps it at a distance for study. While it is held at a distance, one cannot use it personally to make meaning and find direction. To demythologize the cross enables one to learn much about it, but it also cuts one off from the cross as a tool to open the door to the Holy.

The frustration of misusing the cross can sometimes engage the creative process once again to move to another stage where the structures of knowing with the cross become remythologized. Now, however, this is a conscious choice not to demythologize. One has to bracket and not use some of the kinds of knowing available about the cross so it can be used for what it is a symbol of. A child may engage the cross with wonder and find it pointing into the Mystery of God spontaneously. The child does this without choice, but the adult must choose to use the symbol for such a task.

Finally, oneness with the Christ that is beyond words steadies into a customary way of life. The cross and the self are transparent. There is a lived reality that only occasionally needs to be symbolized for oneself, and yet there is a need for community. Community needs a language, so for others and for the need of community, one continues to speak and gesture this oneness with God in Christ by making the sign of the cross and/or bowing to the cross and speaking of it. One also recognizes the responsibility to pass on the spoken and unspoken use of the cross to the young.

As an observer there is much to say about the stages of thinking about the cross. When we ask people what they think about the cross, that is what we hear. There is no way to study what one knows when one is in the cross, meditating. One is not sure until afterward that something has happened and then what is known is not what was known then. The wondering that opened up the creative process to discover new meaning and speak about it was not able to be "languaged."

7. The phrase of Robert Kegan's, "constitutive activity rather than constitutions," comes from his chapter "There the Dance Is: Religious Dimensions of a Developmental Framework" in Christiane Brusselmans, ed., *Toward Moral and Religious Maturity* (Morristown, NJ: Silver Burdett, 1980). Kegan's important book following up on these observations is *The Evolving Self: Problem and Process in Human Development* (Cambridge, MA: Harvard Univ. Press, 1982).

8. See note 2.

9. D. W. Winnicott, *The Maturational Process and the Facilitating Environment* (London: Hogarth Press and Institute of Psycho-Analysis, 1965).

10. Søren Kierkegaard, *The Concept of Dread* (Princeton: Princeton Univ. Press, 1957), p. 38.

11. Reed, *The Dynamics of Religion*, p. 154.
12. Milton Rokeach, *The Open and Closed Mind* (New York: Basic Books, 1960), pp. 67–68.
13. Quoted in Andre Godin, *The Psychological Dynamics of Religious Experience* (Birmingham, AL: Religious Education Press, 1985), p. 252. Godin (p. 251) says: "In psychology, imagination is studied, recognized and interpreted as a vital and productive human capacity. Through imagination we escape from the pressure of circumstances and oppressive situations; we are freed to return in a less anguished state and to modify those conditions that are bad for growth. But it is essential to return and modify them and not get lost in dream languages."

CHAPTER 6. The Imagination and Godly Play

1. Gerhard Von Rad, *Genesis* (Philadelphia: Westminster Press, 1961), p. 23.
2. The survey of the Hebraic and Hellenistic views of the imagination primarily follows the study of Richard Kearney in *The Wake of Imagination: Toward a Postmodern Culture* (Minneapolis: Univ. of Minnesota Press, 1988), pp. 37–113.
3. This is a very rough way of putting this. It is not quite what Garrett Green is saying, but I would like to refer you to his book as an excellent study of these issues: Garrett Green, *Imagining God: Theology and the Religious Imagination* (San Francisco: Harper and Row, 1989).
4. Paul Ricoeur, "L'imagination dans le discours et dans l'action," in *Du texte a l'action: Essais d'herméneutique, II* (Paris: Du Seuil, 1986). Quoted in Kearney, *The Wake of Imagination*, pp. 400–401.
5. Mary Warnock, *Imagination* (Berkeley and Los Angeles: Univ. of California Press, 1976).
6. See note 2.
7. Kearney, *The Wake of Imagination*, p. 11.
8. Melvin Konner, *The Tangled Wing: Biological Constraints on the Human Spirit* (New York: Holt, Rinehart and Winston, 1982).
9. See note 3. For Green's analysis of the three levels, see especially pp. 65–66. Green concludes that only the third level is directly pertinent to theology. The other two levels would in my view be related to religious experience, which in turn is related to theology.
10. Weisberg's study is the primary source for the discussion that follows. Robert W. Weisberg, *Creativity: Genius and Other Myths* (New York: W. H. Freeman, 1986).
11. Graham Wallas, *The Art of Thought* (New York: Harcourt, Brace, 1926).

12. Robert L. Ebel, ed., *Encyclopedia of Educational Research*, 4th ed. (London: Macmillan, 1969), p. 267.
13. James E. Loder, *The Transforming Moment: Understanding Convictional Experiences* (San Francisco: Harper and Row, 1981).
14. James H. Austin, *Chase, Chance and Creativity: The Lucky Art of Novelty* (New York: Columbia Univ. Press, 1978), pp. 137–143.
15. Austin, *Chase, Chance and Creativity*, p. 143.
16. The shift of energy from scanning to articulation is difficult to speak about. Many modern commentators have tried. Efforts to explain the process, however, often seem to be no more than a renaming of the moment of insight. To illustrate this difficulty, some modern attempts to explain the moment of insight follow.

In *Creativity: The Magic Synthesis* (New York: Basic Books, 1976), Silvano Arieti called the moment in the process just before insight a kind of "amorphous cognition" that occurs without representation and that cannot be shared. He coined the term *endocept* to name (but not explain) this. It is the "springboard to creativity." At this point the process breaks into symbols of communication, actions, more definite feelings, images, dreams, fantasies, daydreams, and reveries. Arieti never explained how we get from the amorphous cognition to the symbols.

In *Imagination* (New York: Harper and Row, 1963), Harold Rugg speculated that the imagination is embedded in tensed body movement. All thought flows from the natural language of the imagination, which he suggested is the symbol. Thinking flows in two directions after it leaves its origin in symbols: felt-thought and verbally reasoned thought.

The imagination is complex. Ray L. Hart, in *Unfinished Man and the Imagination* (New York: Herder and Herder, 1968), argued that the imagination is not one power. It is a wide range of mental acts that includes reason and sensation. The meaning that is created is a kind of symbolic meaning that engages the mind as a whole.

In *More Than Meets the Eye: Ritual and Parish Liturgy* (New York/Ramsey: Paulist Press, 1983), Patrick W. Collins said (p. 35) that the imagination not only is complex but is "the crossroads" itself of this complexity. It is the "linking point" of all the faculties. It is *how* we participate in our experience.

William F. Lynch, in *Images of Hope: Imagination as Healer of the Hopeless* (Baltimore: Helican, 1965), also suggested that the imagination is a comprehensive act of the human being. He linked imagination to hope, a sense that "there is a way out." Imagination is how we see the unseen and how we break the bonds of the senses. He said that "the task of the imagination is to imagine the real." One can push "through fantasy and unreality into reality."

This is why Lynch said that the cause of mental illness is a lack of imagination.

The imagination can be used to re-imagine who we are as human beings. It was in such a context that Walter Conn, in *Christian Conversion: A Developmental Integration of Autonomy and Surrender* (New York/Mahwah: Paulist Press, 1986), said "Our concern is the affective, cognitive, moral, and religious totality of the person." The first production of the imagination, the symbol, "actualizes, reveals and influences the multidimensional person in its wholeness." He concluded, "And this is that mode of affective understanding which various theorists name intuitive, imaginative, creative, presentational, gestural felt-thought, and which in this study I will simply call symbolic. It will be central to our interpretation of personal conversion."

In *Introduction to Theology: An Invitation to Reflection upon the Christian Mythos* (Philadelphia: Fortress Press, 1976), Theodore W. Jennings wrote, "Imagination is the initial way in which existence and reality come to expression in such a way as to be available to human awareness and to serve as the legitimate ground of reflection. . . . The function of imagination then is the representation of the patterns of participation in and transcendence of the world in such a way as to make possible the experiencing of, and conscious participation in, reality" (pp. 17–18).

It is difficult to find a way to break down the imagination into its parts or get an "outside" observer's view of it to reflect on in language. We can be open to it and be aware of its movement, but when we seek it as the object of observation it seems to go into hiding. This is why I have settled on a sense of the flow or movement of the process in this book, rather than trying to establish a more static definition like the preceding examples.

17. In addition to the complexity of the imagination itself, there is another complexity related to the kind of product produced. Please see H. Hughes, "Individual and Group Creativity in Science," in M. Coler, ed., *Essays on Creativity in the Sciences* (New York: New York Univ. Press, 1963), pp. 93–101.

Hughes identified seven variations of creativity based on the kind of creative product: *replacement*—providing a new alternative solution to a previous problem; *deliberate invention*—consciously introducing a number of associations and then trying to find some logical connections among them; *recognition of errors*—looking at existing solutions to find out what is wrong and working from there to define new solutions; *routinizing*—reducing a complex recurring problem to a simple routine; *generalizing*—recognizing whole classes of problems that are solvable by known means; *stimulation and release*—stimulating others and releasing creative energies in them even if they are not especially creative themselves; and *collaboration*—extending with ingenuity the ideas of another person.

CHAPTER 7. The Theology of Childhood

1. Edward Robinson, *The Original Vision: A Study of the Religious Experience of Childhood* (Oxford: Religious Experience Research Unit, Manchester College, 1977).
2. Ronald Goldman, *Readiness for Religion: A Basis for Developmental Religious Education* (London: Routledge & Kegan Paul, 1965), pp. 49–50. Reprinted by Seabury Press, New York, 1970.
3. Ronald Goldman, *Religious Thinking from Childhood to Adolescence* (Humanities Press, 1965), p. 14. Orig. pub. 1964. Reprinted by Seabury Press, New York, 1968.
4. David Hay, *Exploring Inner Space: Is God Still Possible in the Twentieth Century?*, rev. ed. (London: Mowbray, 1987).
5. Goldman, *Readiness for Religion*, p. 33, and *Religious Thinking*, p. 226.
6. Robinson, *The Original Vision*, pp. 12–13.
7. C. Daniel Batson and W. Larry Ventis, *The Religious Experience: A Social-Psychological Perspective* (New York and Oxford: Oxford Univ. Press, 1982), p. 132.
8. My approach to pediatric pastoral care was developed about the years 1974–1984 at the Institute of Religion in the Texas Medical Center. Please see especially Jerome W. Berryman's chapters "The Rite of Anointing and the Pastoral Care of Sick Children," in Diane Apostolos-Cappadona, ed., *The Sacred Play of Children* (New York: Seabury Press, 1983) and "The Chaplain's Strange Language: A Unique Contribution to the Health Care Team," in Jan Van Eys, ed., *The Chaplaincy in a Children's Cancer Center* (Austin, TX: Univ. of Texas Press, 1985); also see Berryman, "Religious Images, Sick Children and Health Care," in *Children in Health Care: Ethical Perspectives*, Association for the Care of Children's Health Special Edition (Spring 1981): 19–31.
9. Robinson, *The Original Vision*, pp. 32–33.
10. Robinson, *The Original Vision*, p. 52.
11. Robinson, *The Original Vision*, p. 101.
12. Samuel Terrien, *The Elusive Presence* (San Francisco: Harper and Row, 1978).
13. Dorothy L. Sayers, *The Mind of the Maker* (New York: Harcourt, Brace, 1941). The text I used was that of Meridian Books, 1956. Important chapters from the book can be found in Sayers, *The Whimsical Christian* (New York: Macmillan, 1978).

14. Sayers, *The Mind of the Maker*, p. 147 (Meridian), p. 195 (Macmillan).
15. Gregory of Nyssa, *The Life of Moses*, translation, introduction, and notes by Abraham J. Malherbe and Everett Ferguson (New York/ Ramsey, Toronto: Paulist Press, 1978).
16. Sayers, *the Mind of the Maker*, p. 66.

Index